cincinnati 5

First Person

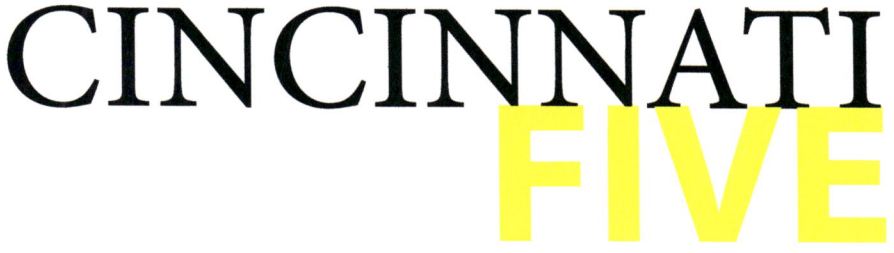

CINCINNATI FIVE

First Person

Emily Moores

TABLE OF CONTENTS

cincinnati FIVE

History is made through documentation. From political upheaval to status updates, documentation dictates who we remember and how. Those who write the documents wield the power to illustrate society. This means, historically, the contributions of women and people of color have been overlooked or omitted. The collaborative nature of the Internet, however, has changed the very nature of documentation, allowing a truer look at who we are.

This is my second book in what I hope to be a long-term project documenting artists integral to Cincinnati's community. My aim is to document and empower local artists. I want this book to pave a path by which the community finds its artists. With the Internet in our pockets, Cincinnati galleries are no further than a Google search. The artists who fill them, though, are not so easily tracked. I hope this book serves as a document, not to galleries, but to the artists themselves.

Each of these Cincinnati Five use documentation in their art. Either through documentation of their process or use of physical documents in their art, these artists write their own place in history.

The selection process for the Cincinnati Five included a panel of three judges. From their fifty initial nominations, the judges selected five artists. There was no set application process. Instead, selection criteria heavily emphasized community engagement. Those chosen were required to have a serious art practice with a minimum of five years exhibition experience. Notoriety and name recognition held zero sway; this project's sole focus is illuminating serious artists integral to the spirit of Cincinnati art.

This project was a massive undertaking. There aren't the words or space on this page to truly express gratitude to the many people who helped form the Cincinnati 5.

Thank you to Matt Distel, Catherine Richards, Sara Waddell Vance, Dan Murphy, Keith Good, Elizabeth Tussey, Anh Tran and Daniel Beach. I am also especially grateful to Modern Makers for hosting the exhibition.

Emily Moores

INTRODUCTION

Cincinnati has a plethora of artistic talent. Institutions like DAAP and the Art Academy have produced incredible, wide-ranging artists proud to call Cincinnati home. Though a collector of contemporary art regardless of medium or location, I love supporting our local talent. Not because I feel compelled to, but because, quite honestly, our local artists are rock stars. I'm proud to call many of them friends. The vast majority of our local artists deserve national representation and renown.

My good friend, Cincinnati art maven Phyllis Weston, once said I, like her, have an eye for great art and great talent. I often think my eye for our tremendous local talent came from her. I am continually amazed by this year's Cincinnati Five. They are an all-star cast of women artists… Tracy Featherstone, Alice Pixley Young, Carolyn Mazloomi, Sheida Soleimani and Carol Tyler. I admire how artists often act as social revolutionaries, highlighting injustices and challenging traditional points of view. It is my hope that this year's Cincinnati 5 will do as much for you. They all impact our community!

Sara Vance Waddell
Art Collector

the panel

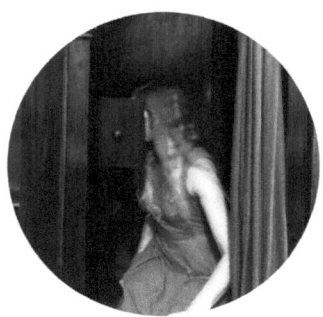

Catherine Elizabeth Richards is an artist and architect. She explores materials and perception on a variety of scales, from wearable art to sculpture and installation, along with citywide interventions. Richards worked at OMA and REX architects in New York City, along with Metaphor Unlimited in London. As an architect, Catherine believes that play and engagement are critical to placemaking. Her studio practice and nonprofit works are process-oriented, with a strategy of critical naiveté. Catherine founded the nationally recognized program Future Blooms, a model for abandoned buildings adopted by several other US cities. She is co-founder of the art collective Hark + Hark and the experimental arts program Modern Makers.

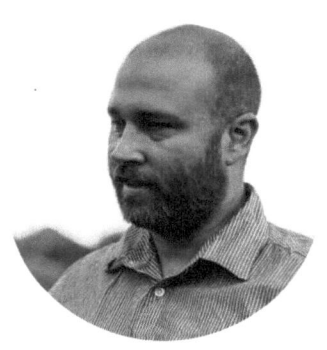

Matt Distel is the Exhibitions Director for The Carnegie in Covington, KY and concurrently serves as an Adjunct Curator of Contemporary Art for the Cincinnati Art Museum. Prior to joining the The Carnegie, Distel was Executive Director of Visionaries + Voices and the co-founder and director of Country Club, a commercial gallery based in Cincinnati and Los Angeles. A Cincinnati native, Distel has been organizing exhibitions since 1994 with a particular focus on artists from the region. From 2003-2007 he was the Associate Curator with the Contemporary Arts Center in Cincinnati. Distel has curated and organized numerous exhibitions and installations including projects with SIMPARCH, Kendell Geers, Guy Ben-ner, Katerina Burin, Temporary Services, The Yes Men, Beth Campbell, Alexis Rockman, Jay Bolotin, Shana Moulton, Future Retrieval, Terry Berlier, Design 99, Courttney Cooper, Lisi Raskin, Ryan McGinness, Ellen Berkenblit, Edie Harper, Tom Wesselmann and Atlas Group.

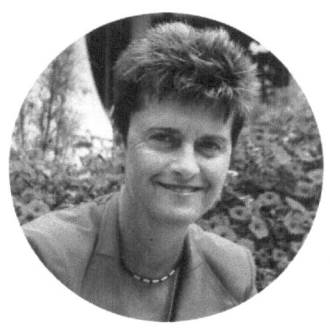

Sara Vance Waddell is the CEO/Owner of SMV Media, a media management company. She has over 30 years of Media Planning and Buying experience. She graduated in 1984 from Morehead State University with a BA in Journalism. Sara currently sits on The Carnegie Board of Directors as Vice President, Artworks as Trustee Emeritus, Ohio Citizens for the Arts, Arts Midwest and Cancer Family Care as Lifetime Trustee. She previously served on The Ohio Arts Council (appointed by Governor Ted Strickland), the Cincinnati Art Museum and Contemporary Arts Center, where she now is a docent. Sara Vance Waddell was selected Enquirer Woman of the Year, 2010, received the Civic Leadership Award from Venue Magazine in 2011, Justin Friedman Presidents Award from Cancer Family Care in 2011, Heart for the Arts Award in 2007 from Learning Through Art. Sara is an avid wine and contemporary art collector.

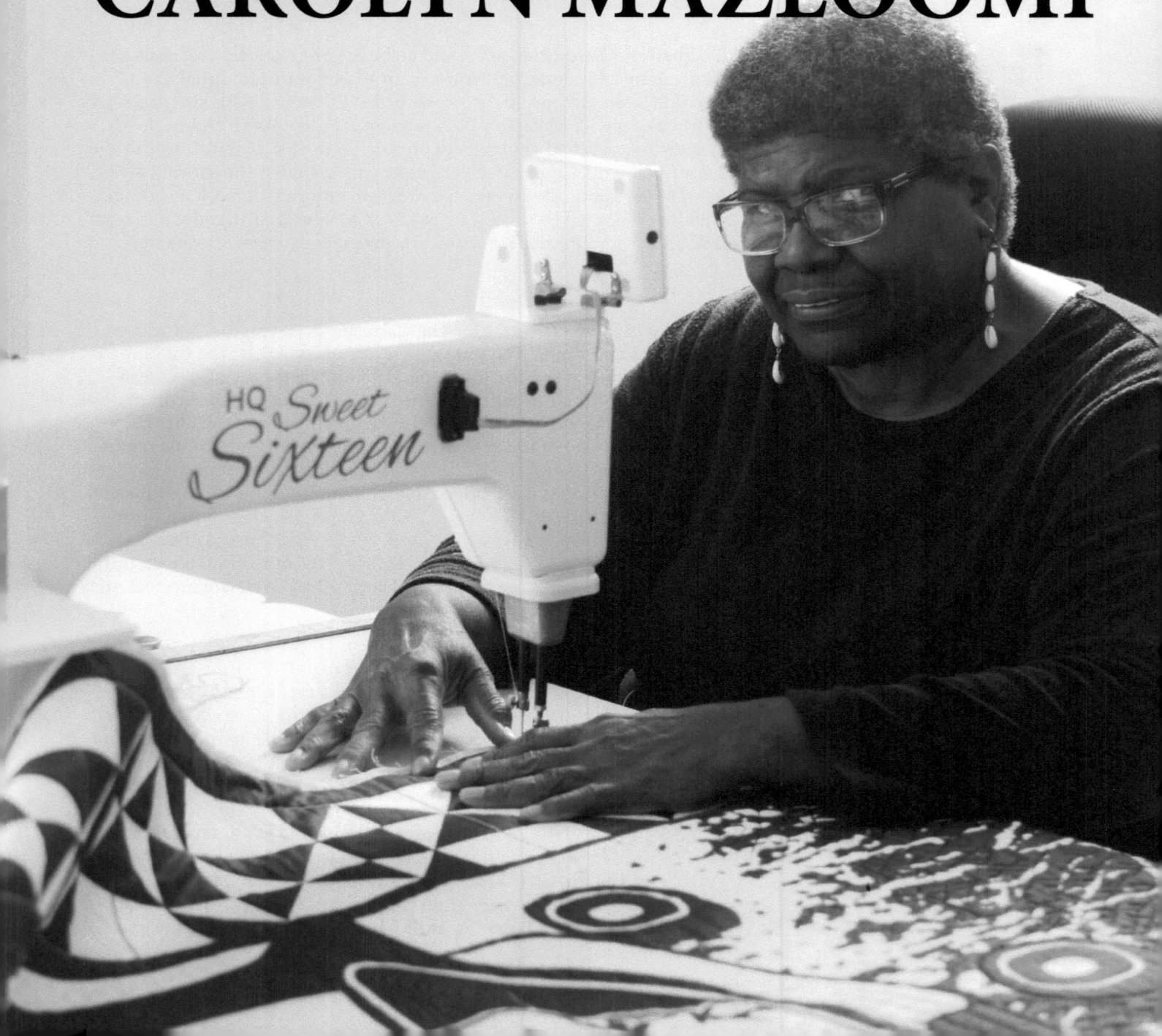

CAROLYN MAZLOOMI

Carolyn Mazloomi is a 21st Century Renaissance woman. Her career started in aerospace engineering and has transitioned into quilting. Born in Baton Rouge, Louisiana, the power of planes enchanted a young Mazloomi. This passion for flight led to a career in aerospace engineering. Undergrad studies at Northrop University in Inglewood, California and a 1985 Ph.D. from the University of Southern California led Mazloomi to her first job with Lockheed Aircraft Company in Los Angeles in research and development. Her final job in the field was that of a crash site investigator for the Federal Aviation Administration.

A trip to Dallas in the early 1970s proved pivotal for Mazloomi. Scouring a Dallas market for items to sell in a gift store she ran on the side, Mazloomi became mesmerized by an Appalachian quilt. She taught herself traditional quilting and began her art career. From traditional quilting techniques, Mazloomi gradually transitioned to art quilts. Mazloomi has long said that, "quilts have jumped off the bed and onto the wall."

Mazloomi not only creates quilts, but also founded an organization to support quiltmakers: the African American Guild of Los Angeles. After the birth of her two children, Mazloomi and her husband moved to Cincinnati. Though her husband had job offers in several different locations, Mazloomi liked the schools in Cincinnati. She saw Cincinnati as a place to raise her children.

Once in Cincinnati, Mazloomi left her previous profession to create art full-time. In 1985, she formed a new organization, the Women of Color Quilters Network (WCQN). The WCQN currently boasts over 1,700 members worldwide. Through the WCQN, Mazloomi works to champion women's causes. She sees the WCQN as an avenue for members to sell their work and sustain their families. Every WCQN exhibition curated by Mazloomi has sold every quilt.

Mazloomi has written a companion book to each exhibition she's curated, now eleven in total. The most recent exhibition, "And Still We Rise," opened at the Freedom Center in 2014. The exhibition was intended to start a conversation about race. The show has proved popular, receiving rave reviews from coast to coast. Mazloomi quilts to tell stories. Her work especially focuses on women and the underprivileged. Though originally working in full color, Mazloomi has transitioned to quilting in black and white. She feels the stark palette emboldens her narratives. To ensure clarity of narrative, Mazloomi writes explanations to each of her art quilts.

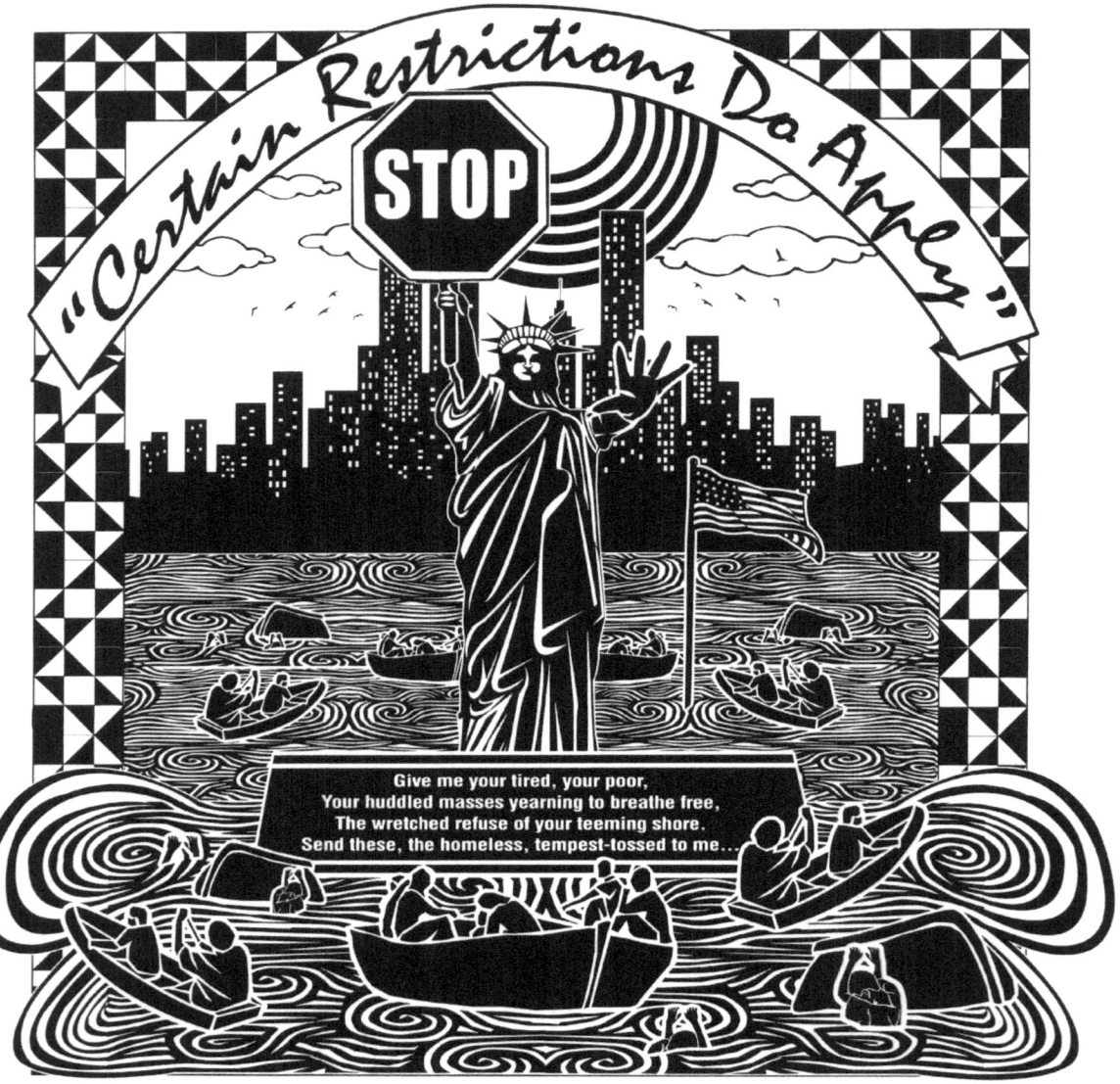

Certain Restrictions Do Apply, 2013
Hand painted, stencil, Tsukineko ink, printed, and machine quilted, 62" x 54"

Xenophobia and racism are alive and well when examining immigration reform in the United States. The discussion has polarized city and states, confounded politicians, and the ordinary citizen. It's an uncomfortable truth: the policy discussion surrounding who deserves to be let into our country is pervasively exclusive. As long as America's boundaries align with divisions of race, class, culture and wealth, our immigration policies will always be racialized social wangling. Immigration policy is never "neutral", regardless of the country.

Certain Restrictions Do Apply honors the many Haitian immigrants who have drown seeking the freedom to live in the United States.

Cincinnati | 8

An Interview with Carolyn

Emily Moores (EM): When you are making the quilts are they depicting a specific story?

Carolyn Mazloomi (CM): They are a specific story. This is about the UN peacekeepers in Africa raping the African girls and leaving behind all of these mixed race babies.

EM: Are you always telling stories?

CM: Always telling stories and always trying to make a difference. Everything should serve a purpose. I can't function if things don't have a purpose. What is the point?

EM: Do you jump around with topics?

CM: I work on several pieces at a time. I do a lot of research because I write a story for each piece. Each quilt has a storyline.

EM: Is the style of your quilts historical?

CM: All of them have a circle around the sun. It is symbolic of unity and continuing of life. You will find that in all my quilts. You will find the sun, and you will find these circles.

EM: Do you always keep the pattern around the edges?

CM: Yes. Because, it is an homage to the traditional quilt makers that have come before with the traditional quilt skills.

I don't do color anymore. It was a transition over the last several years. I don't like working in color. I am not a colorist, and it takes so much time to audition the fabric. It takes weeks for me. I could have been finished with the quilt. Plus, black and white is dramatic. There is nothing between the audience and the message you want to convey. It is very stark. I love black and white, and I will never do color again.

I was contacted by the set designer for the movie [*The Hateful Eight* directed by Quentin Tarantino], who was familiar with my work. She commissioned two quilts for the movie set. The movie was set in the late 1800s in the west, and the quilts were to be used on beds of a boarding house. They had to look like rustic, utilitarian quilts from the period. I was shipped lots of antique denim and antique repurposed linen feed sacks to use to construct the pieces.

EM: What is your process to start a show? Does something touch you and you build on it?

CM: Exactly. I curated a show about the history of jazz in African American culture. I love jazz. Jazz is an intricate part of the Black experience, here, in this country. If you ask curators or historians, what are the most iconic art forms in the country, they would say jazz and quilts. Those are two unique African American expressions that contributed to history in the United States. It is all a good marriage between the two, jazz and quilts. The show was smoking. It was talking. It was playing its own music.

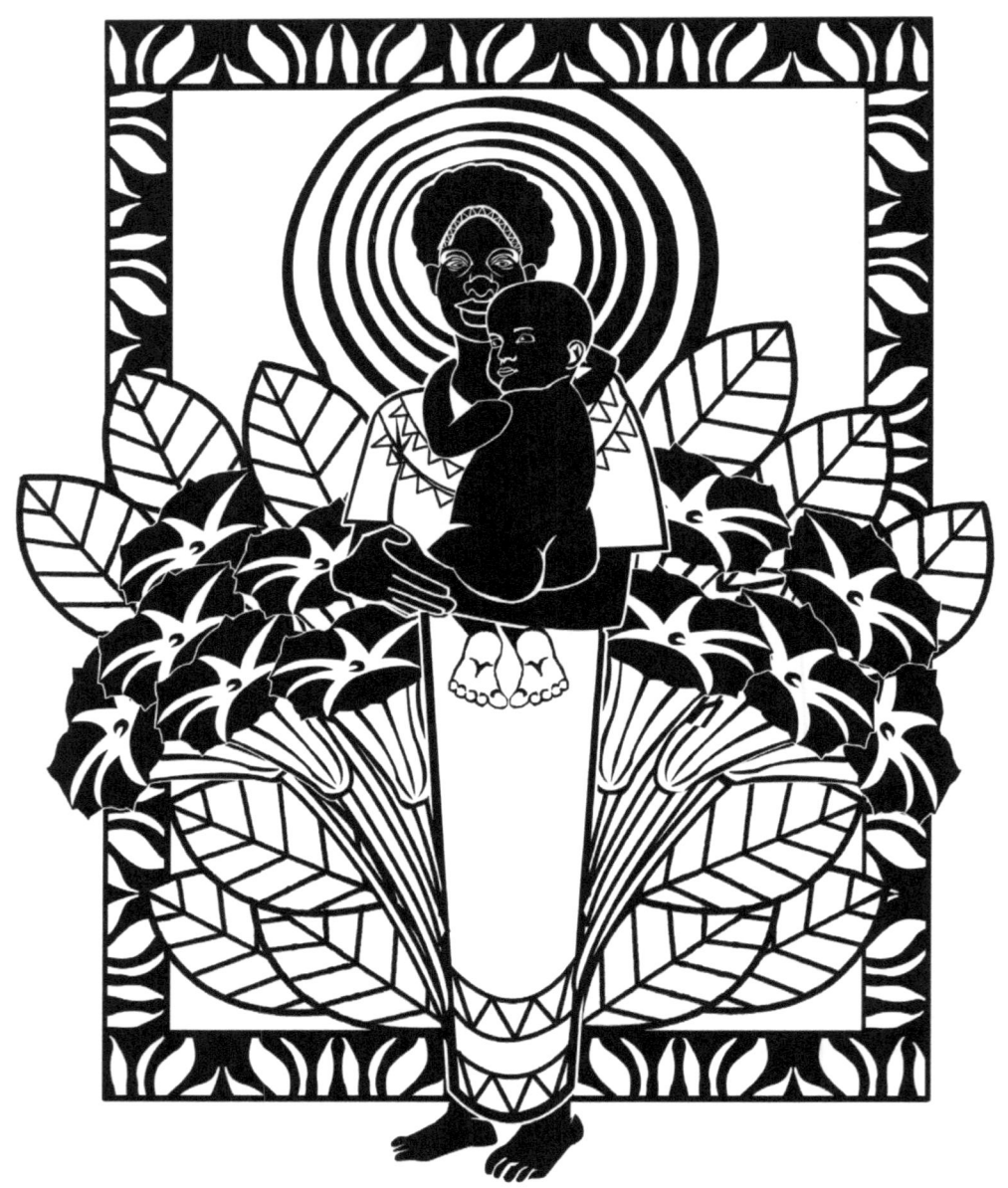

Precious, 2013
Hand painted, stencil, Tsukineko ink, printed, and machine quilted, 72" x 60"

"Precious" honors the sacred station of mothers. As first teachers of their children, they have the capacity to influence every human being on the planet.

Cincinnati | 10

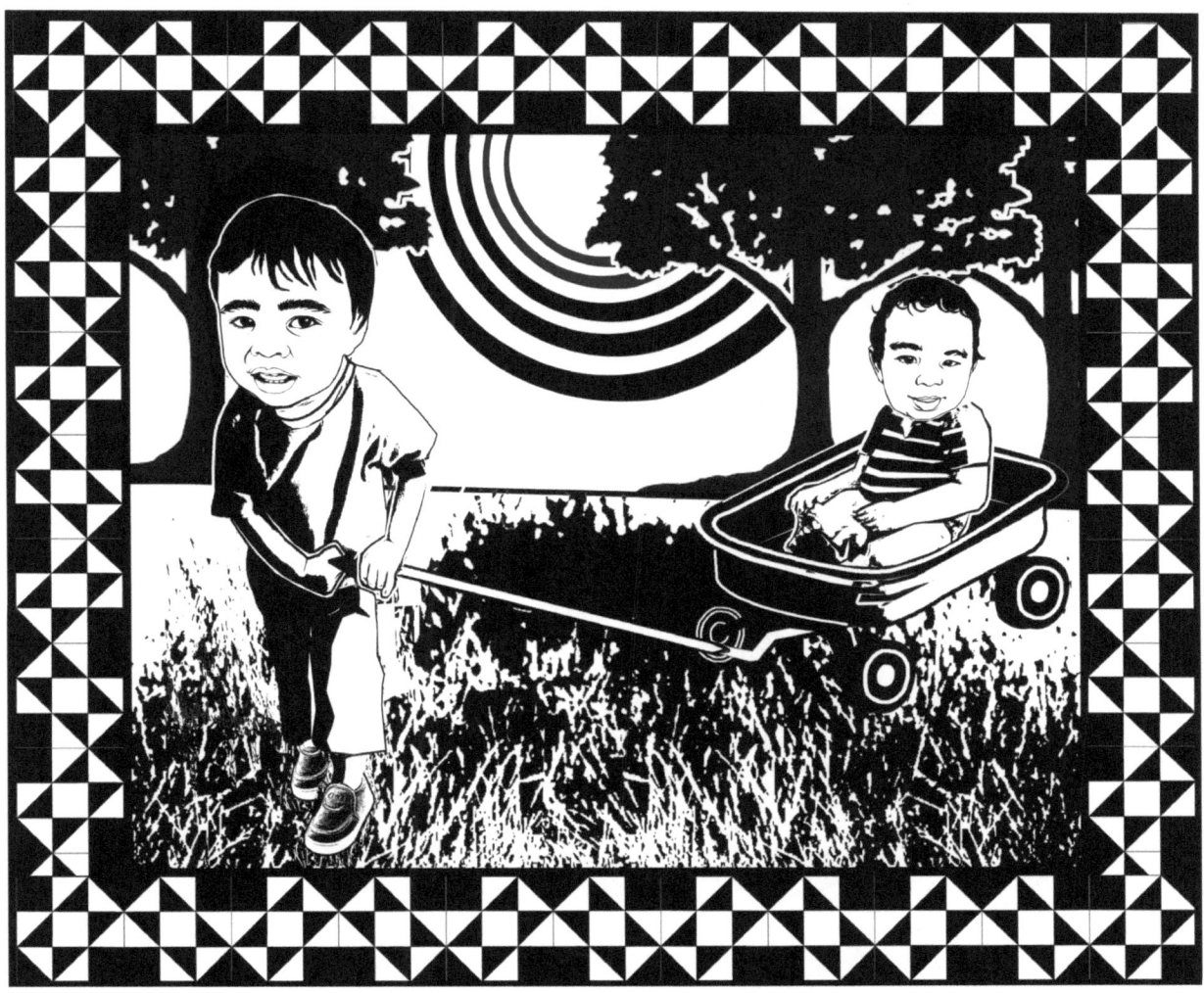

I Am My Brother's Keeper, 2016
Hand painted, stencil, Tsukineko ink, printed, and machine quilted, 61" x 74"

Brothers can sit in the same room, in silence, yet know how the other feels. It's picking up right where you left off, even if it's been weeks, months or years since the last deep conversation. It's the knowledge that, at the end of the day, you'll always be able to call on that person for support.

My eldest grandson loves his role as "big brother" to his younger sibling. Hopefully the relationship they forge together will last a lifetime. I wish for them to always be closest allies, and be able to bridge the gaps of their individual personalities and interests. They should inspire each other to be the best they can be.

The brothers will never know another human being for as long as they know each other.

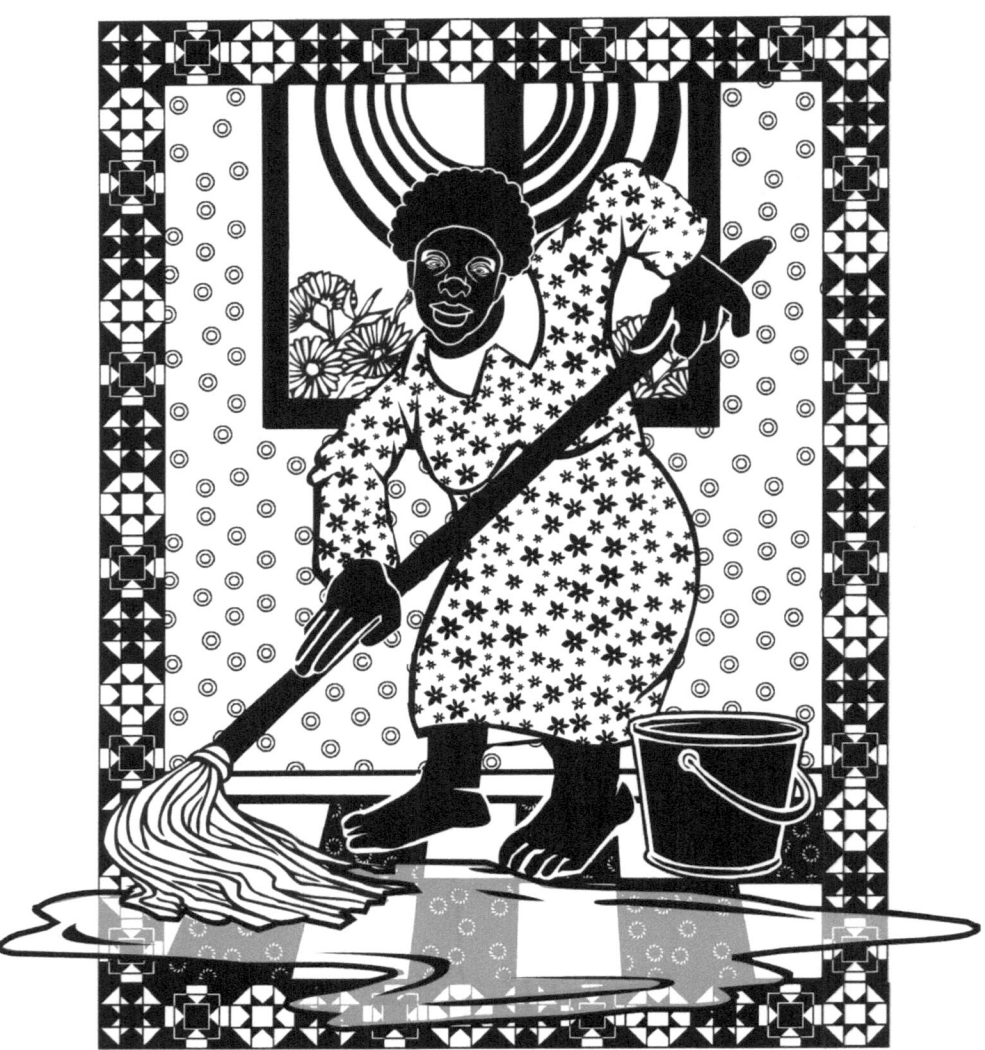

Maid in America, 2013
Hand painted, stencil, Tsukineko ink, printed, and machine quilted, 58" x 47"

Maid in America pays homage to the African American maids working in the South during the Civil Rights Movement. At the time over ninety percent of African American women worked as maids. They contributed significantly to the era by participating in the Montgomery, Alabama bus boycott. The women refused to ride the buses as protest against the jailing of Rosa Parks for her refusing to give up her bus seat to a white man. The protest took place from December 5, 1955, to December 20, 1956. The boycott is regarded as the first large-scale demonstration against segregation in the U.S. The boycott of public buses by blacks in Montgomery began on the day of Parks' court hearing and lasted 381 days. The U.S. Supreme Court ultimately ordered Montgomery to integrate its bus system. It was at this time Rev. Martin Luther King, Jr. emerged as a prominent national leader of the American civil rights movement in the wake of the action.

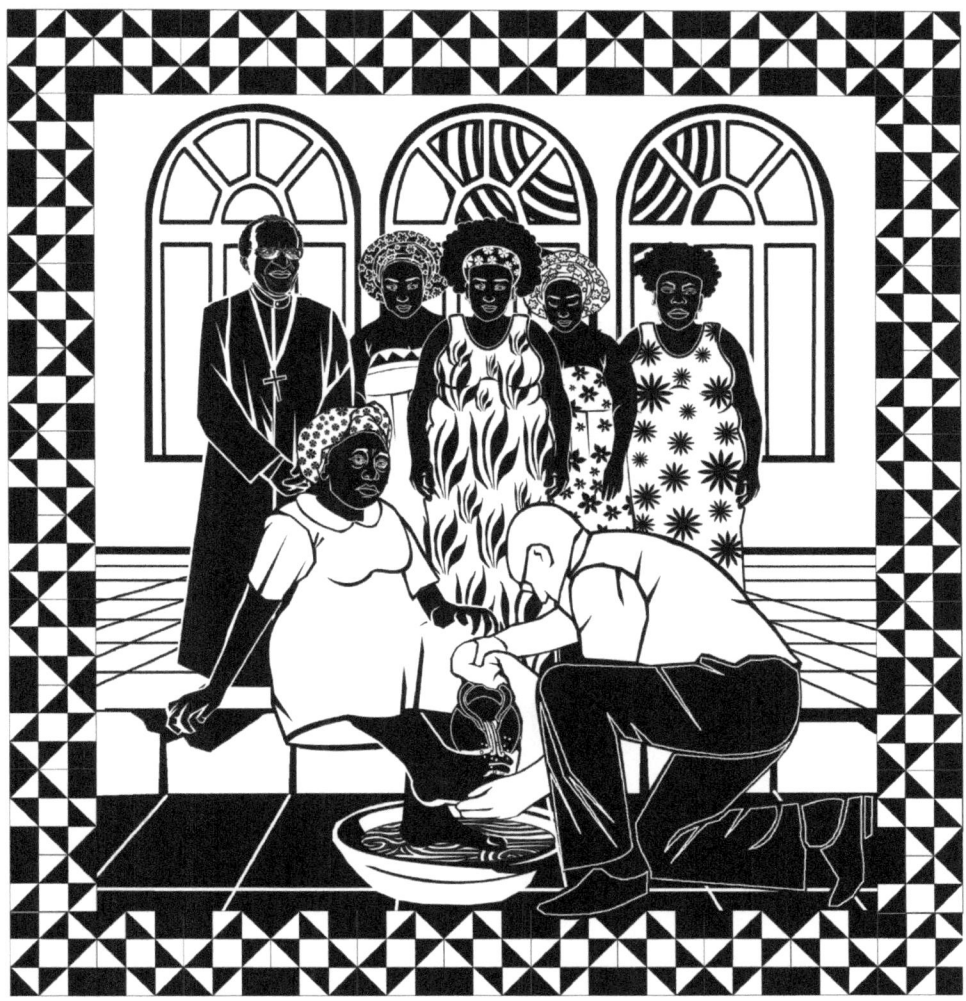

In the Spirit of Forgiveness, 2014
Hand painted, stencil, Tsukineko ink, printed, and machine quilted, 58" x 58"

Adriaan Johannes Vlok was Minister of Law and Order in South Africa from 1986 to 1991 during the final years of the apartheid era. He helped to plan and implement the death of thousands of anti-apartheid activists. In 1999, Vlok became a pariah among white South Africans when he became the only cabinet minister to appear before the Truth and Reconciliation Commission to admit committing crimes against blacks. He has granted amnesty by the Truth and Reconciliation Commission, which was set up to help the nation come to terms with its past. Bishop Desmond Tutu is a member of the Commission. As atonement for his despicable acts, Vlok washed the feet of 10 black South African women--mothers whose young sons were brutally murdered by the police under his watch in the 1980s.

To wash the feet of another human being is one of the most humbling things one can ever do.

13

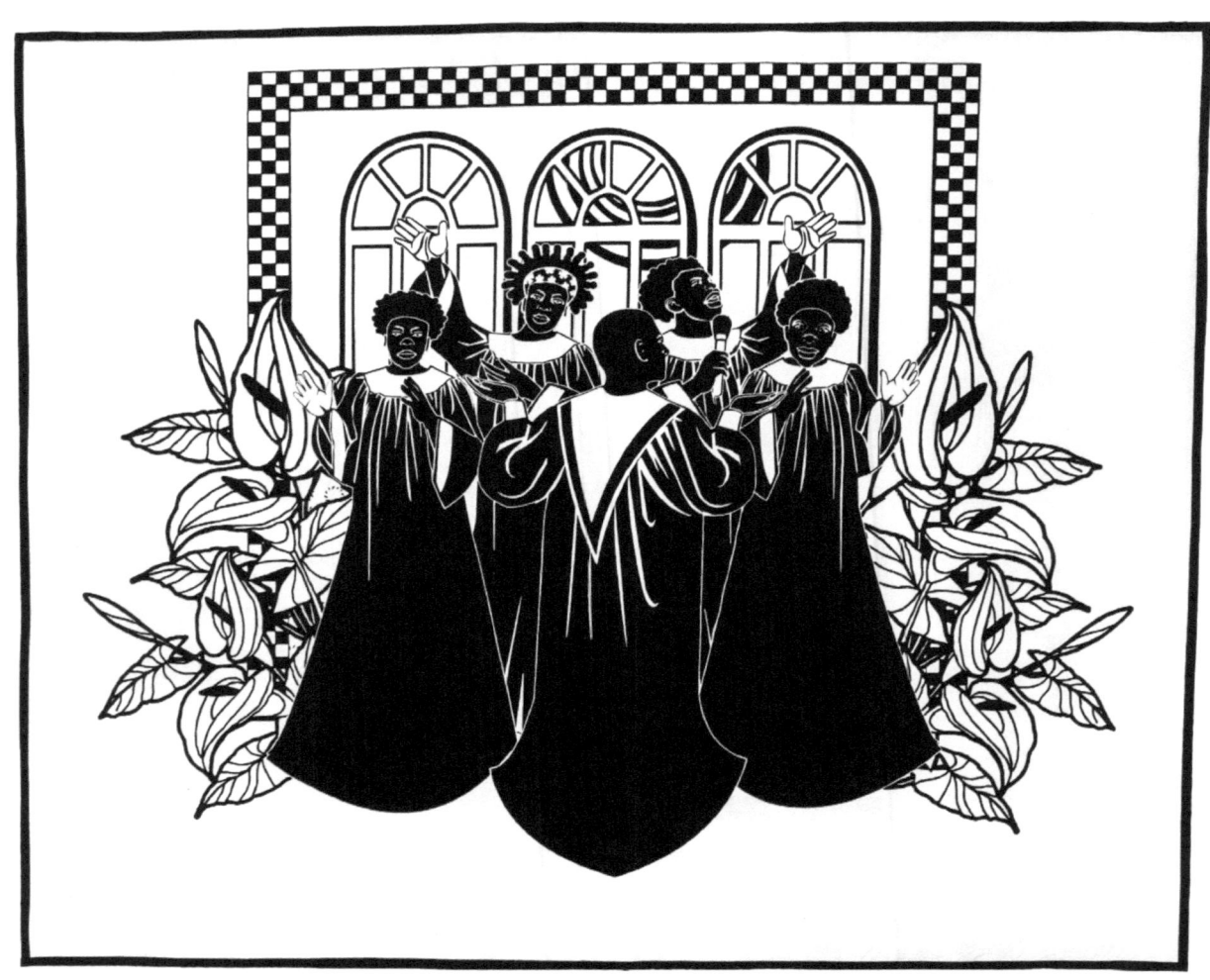

Singing Praises to the Lord, 2013
Hand painted, stencil, Tsukineko ink, printed, and machine quilted, 49" x 64"

"Negro spirituals" in their words and in the way they are performed musically exemplify the deep religious feelings of the African American people. They are an important part of the American cultural heritage, and are now recognized globally as anthems to liberty that can feed the deepest aspirations of the human soul. The great majority of Negro spirituals are very old. In a lot of cases the tunes and rhythms are so ancient they can trace them back to Africa. The songs were all solely based off the hard times African Americans were going through during slavery. African Americans used these spirituals to stay in tuned to their faith to be the guidance through a hard time such as slavery. I enjoy these old hymns, for they are indeed spiritual soul food.

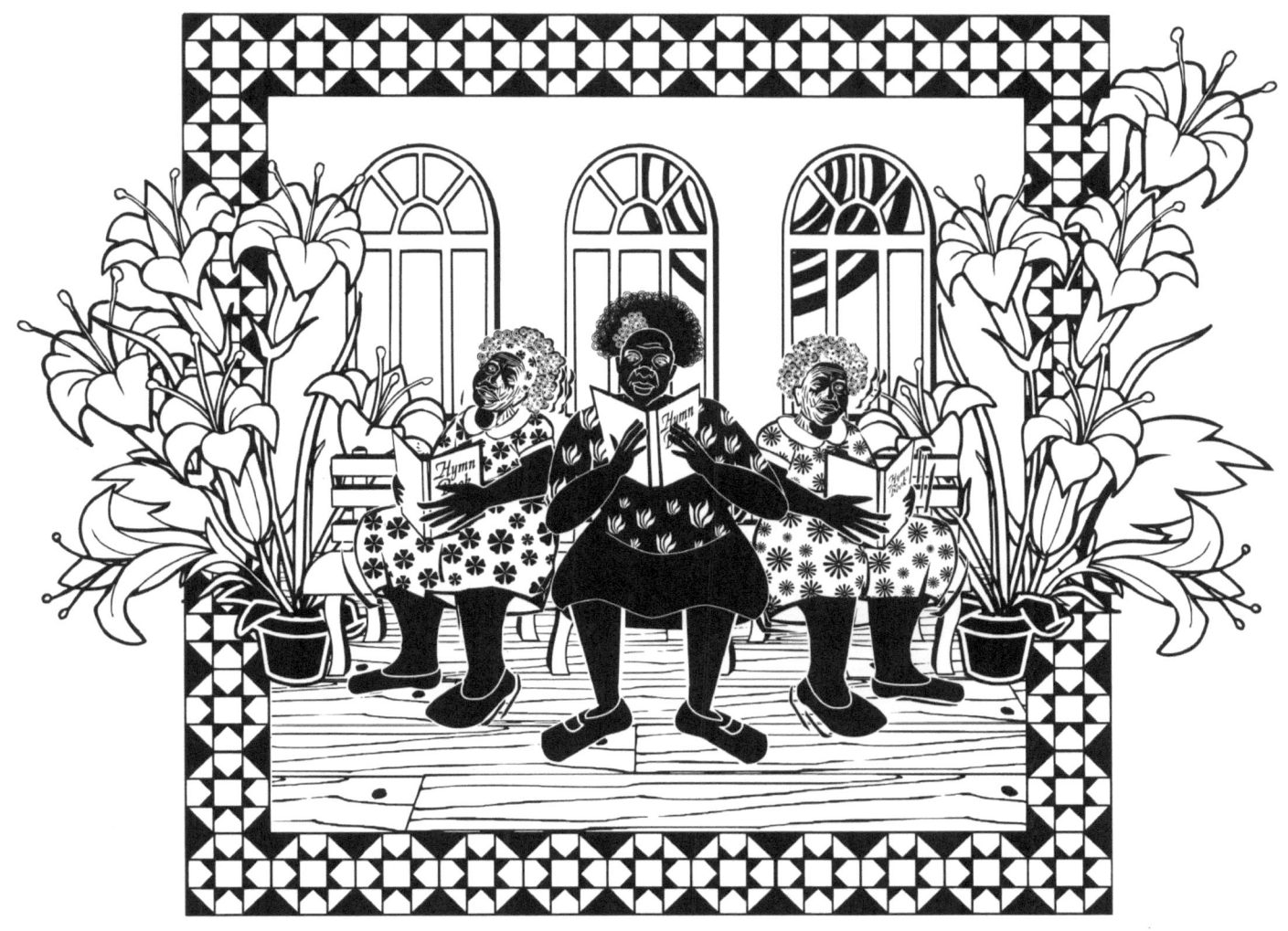

Gimme that Old Time Religion, 2013
Hand painted, stencil, Tsukineko ink, printed, and machine quilted, 62" x 75"

This work celebrates the women in my family...strong women with deep spiritual beliefs. Perhaps the most profound echoes of African culture through-out the Diaspora are to be found in religious tradition. The message of salvation and the unconditional love of God have always been powerful draws for African Americans. Religion and spirituality provide a foundation for coping by extending a personal relationship with God. The church provides the benefit of participation in a social network of church members who became important sources of practical aid and emotional support.

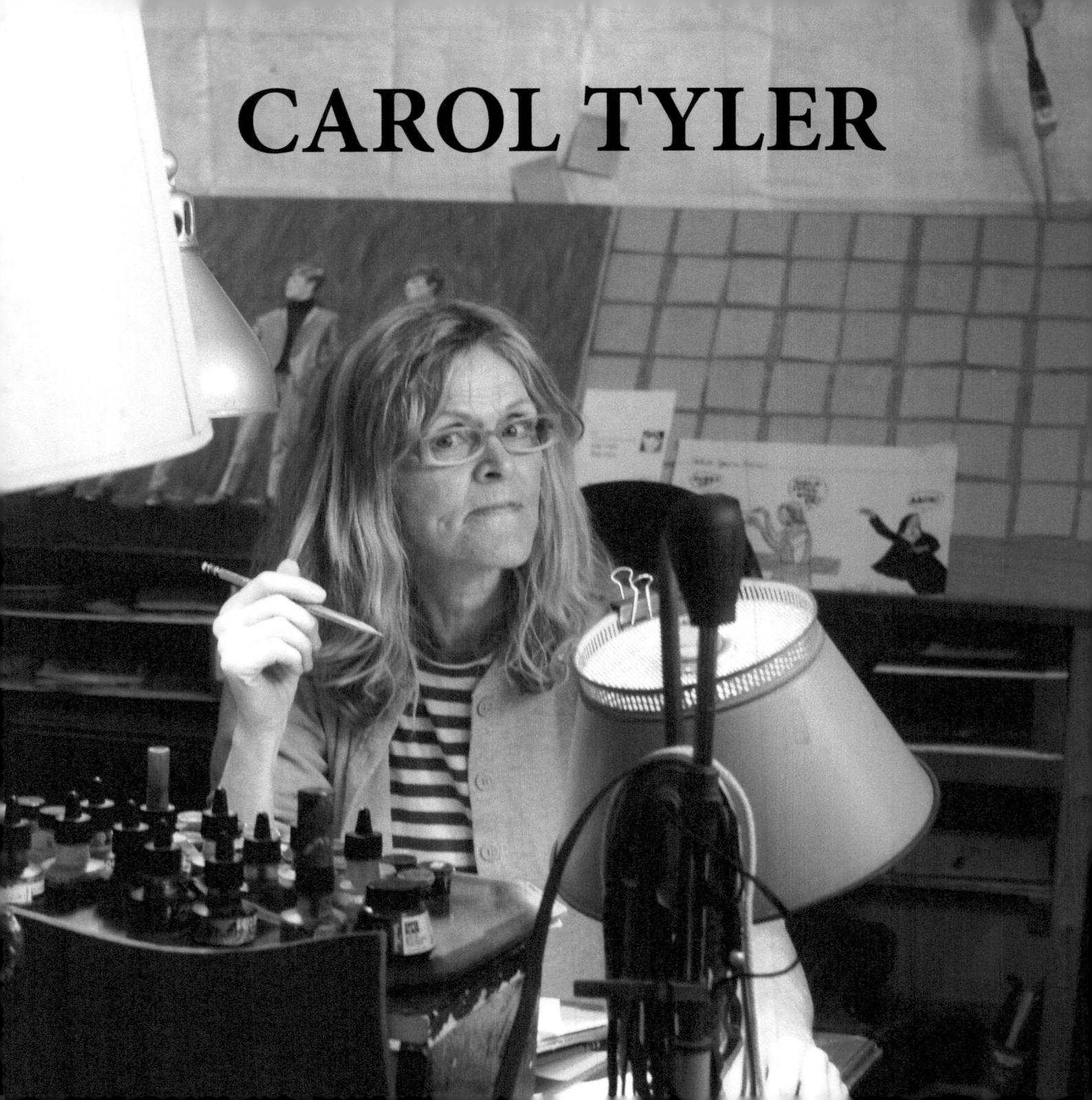

CAROL TYLER

Carol Tyler's illustrated narratives meditate on her life. Much of her work delves into her personal struggles. Her family was forged in the furnaces of World War II. The war drew her urban pipefitter father from Chicago to rural Tennessee, where he met Tyler's mother. As a child, Tyler found her parents idiosyncratic, distant and fascinating. They behaved apart from other children's parents.

Carol Tyler was born in Chicago after the war. Though not artists, Tyler found her parents eminently artful. Her mother was witty, with a flair for handwriting. Her father was a skilled craftsman and plumber. Neither, however, was emotionally accessible. The trauma of war haunted her father. Her mother lost a child early in their marriage. The complexity and hardship of her parents' 67-year marriage intrigues Tyler. She uses her comic stories as a way to make sense of her inner demons, often by depicting the lives of her parents.

Tyler is a born storyteller. As an undergrad at Middle Tennessee State University, her artwork spun concrete imagery into stories. She would tell her classmates the story behind each image. Carol Tyler's discovery of image and story, however, coincided with the rise of Abstract Expressionism and Post-Painterly Abstraction. Emptiness was in vogue. Recognizable imagery was not acceptable in art. As a grad student at Syracuse University, a visiting artist proclaimed Tyler's use of recognizable imagery meant she'd never produce a masterpiece.

Only after school, upon moving to California, did Tyler find a home in the Post Underground Comix scene. She developed friendships with those, like her, who used their personal lives to tell stories. She loved how autobiographical comics were both intimate and intense. Her ability to draw representationally and tell stories made autobiographical comics a natural fit. As she established her career, Tyler also made some advancements in her personal life: she became a mother.

Unfortunately, her marriage crumbled. She and her twelve-year-old daughter needed a fresh start. Tyler went to a US map, closed her eyes and jabbed her finger. She sold everything she owned, and in 1997, with only $1,000 to her name, Carol Tyler moved to where her finger landed: Cincinnati.

Once Tyler's daughter left for college, she got back to comics full-time. She published an acclaimed book called *Late Bloomer*. It was a collection of everything she had created as a mother. Soon after, Tyler took a job teaching at UC. The past decade has seen her repeatedly teach one class: Comics, Graphic Novels, and Sequential Art. Tyler strives to make well-rounded students, full of the life translates to good art. After all, cartoonists need very little to create: a pencil and the back of an envelope can be magical.

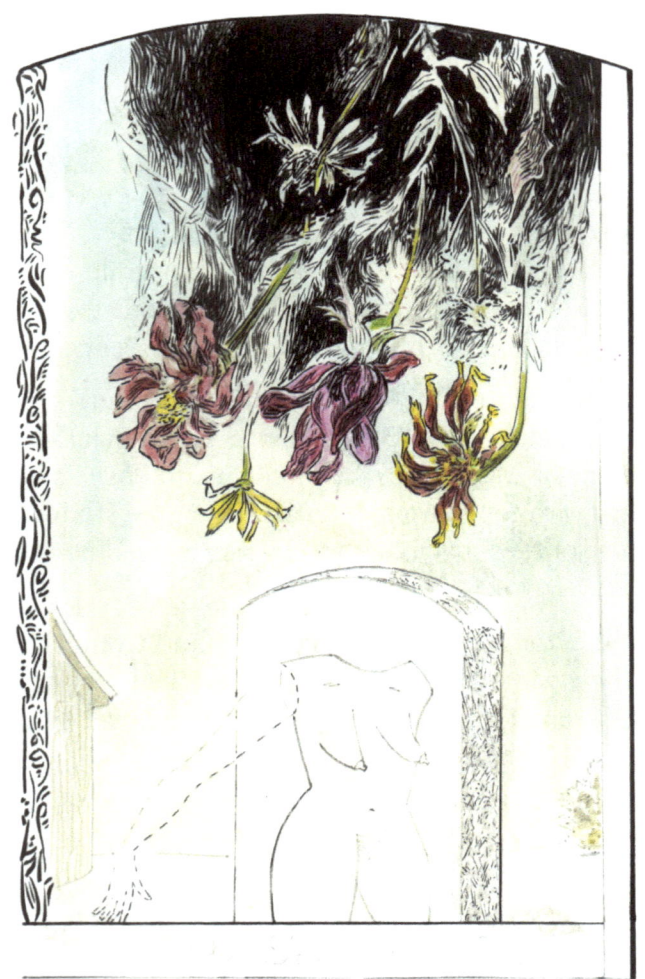
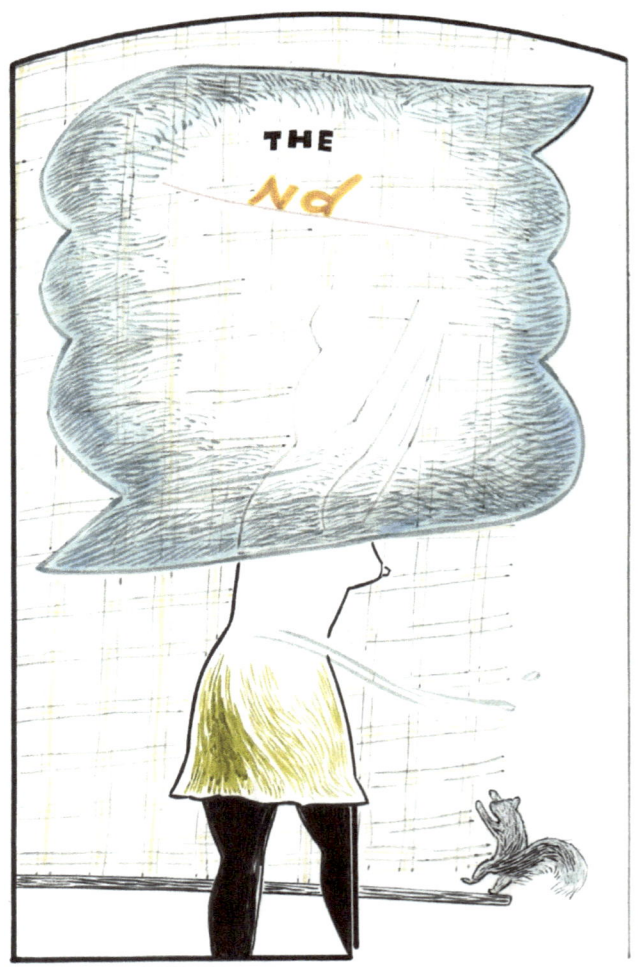

Grief Art, 2014
Ink on paper, 7" x 10"

An Interview with Carol

Emily Moores (EM): Your artwork is autobiographical and focuses on everyday life. Why is it important to focus on those issues?

Carol Tyler (CT): It is all here in everyday life, if you are awake to it. I just see beauty in everyday things. I see sadness, too. All range of experiences that humans have just unfolds all the time, every day, with a kernel of sadness in the middle. So, it is interesting. I have always done autobiographical work. My next book is about sadness, grief, and mourning. I lost a bunch of people in a short amount of time, and it is at the heart of everything I experience these days. So, of course, it is going to become art. Of course, I use humor and wit because, like I said, I see beauty in everything. The joining of all these emotions is my artistic driver.

EM: Do comic books create a sense of intimacy that you are attracted to, versus making paintings?

CT: I think that they both have that potential. When you are telling something very revealing and personal and people have to linger with that, spend time reading it, that is an intimate connection. When you walk into an art gallery, I notice that people don't spend a lot of time with the work in general, but people spend a lot of time with my work because they have to read it.

I had the blessing of the one person show [January 2016 at the Meyers Gallery]. I tried to create a space that people would linger in. It was very moving for people to be able to stand there and read. See all my art work. I had it set up where you could walk through my head. I wrote on the wall so you could linger longer. There were themes, like grief,

inspiration, distraction, and so on...

I don't know about just having painting after painting. Just a single panel. I visit it a lot in my brain. I hope that I have time on this earth to knock out some great ideas. I was in Italy this summer. I got to see some Gothic art. I am missing that for storytelling.

I am a maker, and I kinda just feel life and then I try to make that the thing. When I have space to work with, I am going to engage the space.

EM: You have an intimate medium of a book. Then you are also drawing everything by hand and telling very personal stories. Do you feel like staying with hand-drawn versus creating on the computer?

CT: I see the computer as an editing tool, not a creating tool. I write on the computer, but no artwork. I have to have the physical sensation of the paint or the pencil. Ooh I smeared. What is most important to me is getting the expression right. Tapping into it and bringing it out. As long as I tap into it, I trust the outcome.

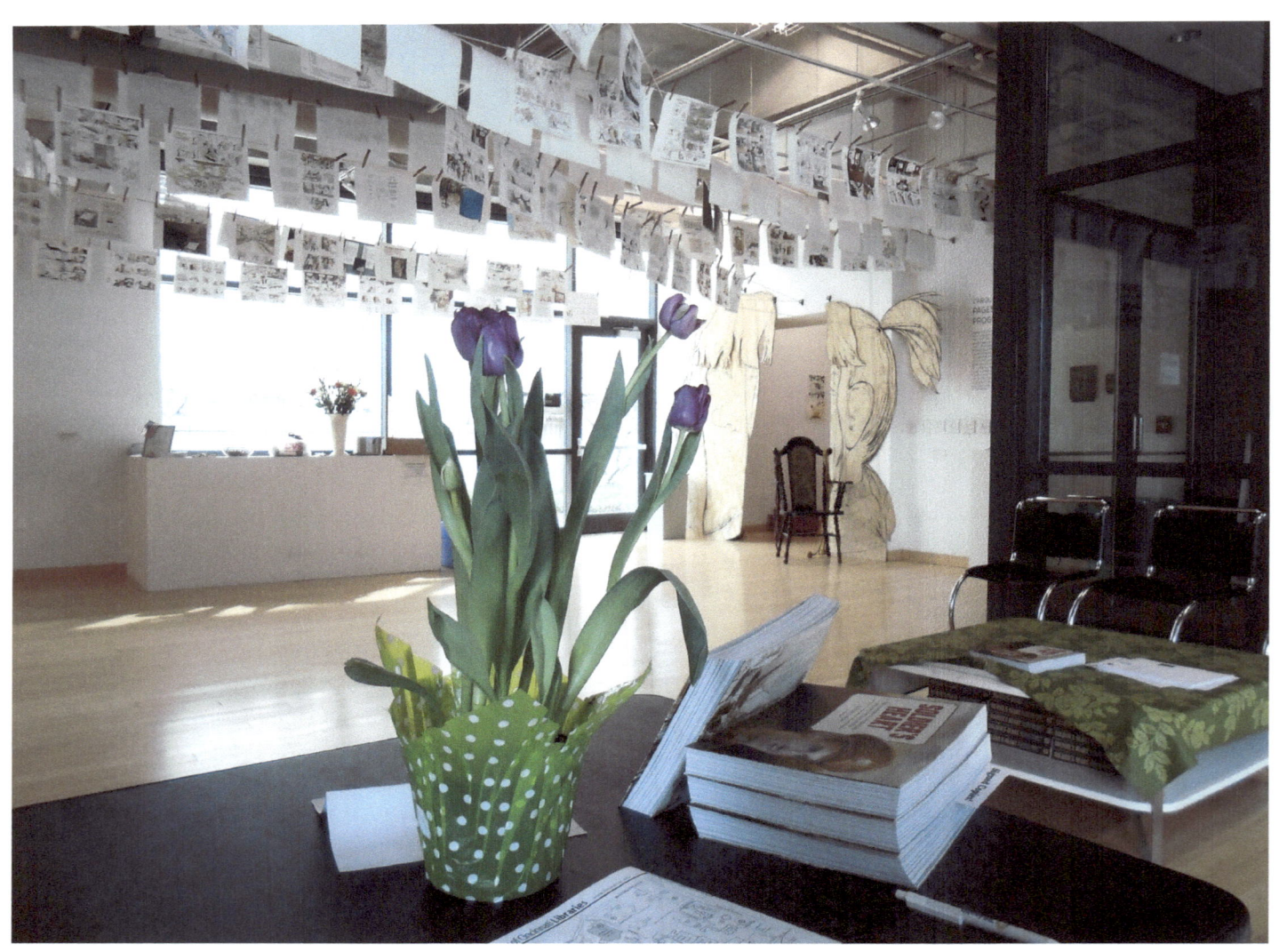

Pages and Process, 2016
The Philip M. Meyers, Jr. Memorial Gallery
Mixed media (pages in photo from *Soldier's Heart*), Dimensions vary

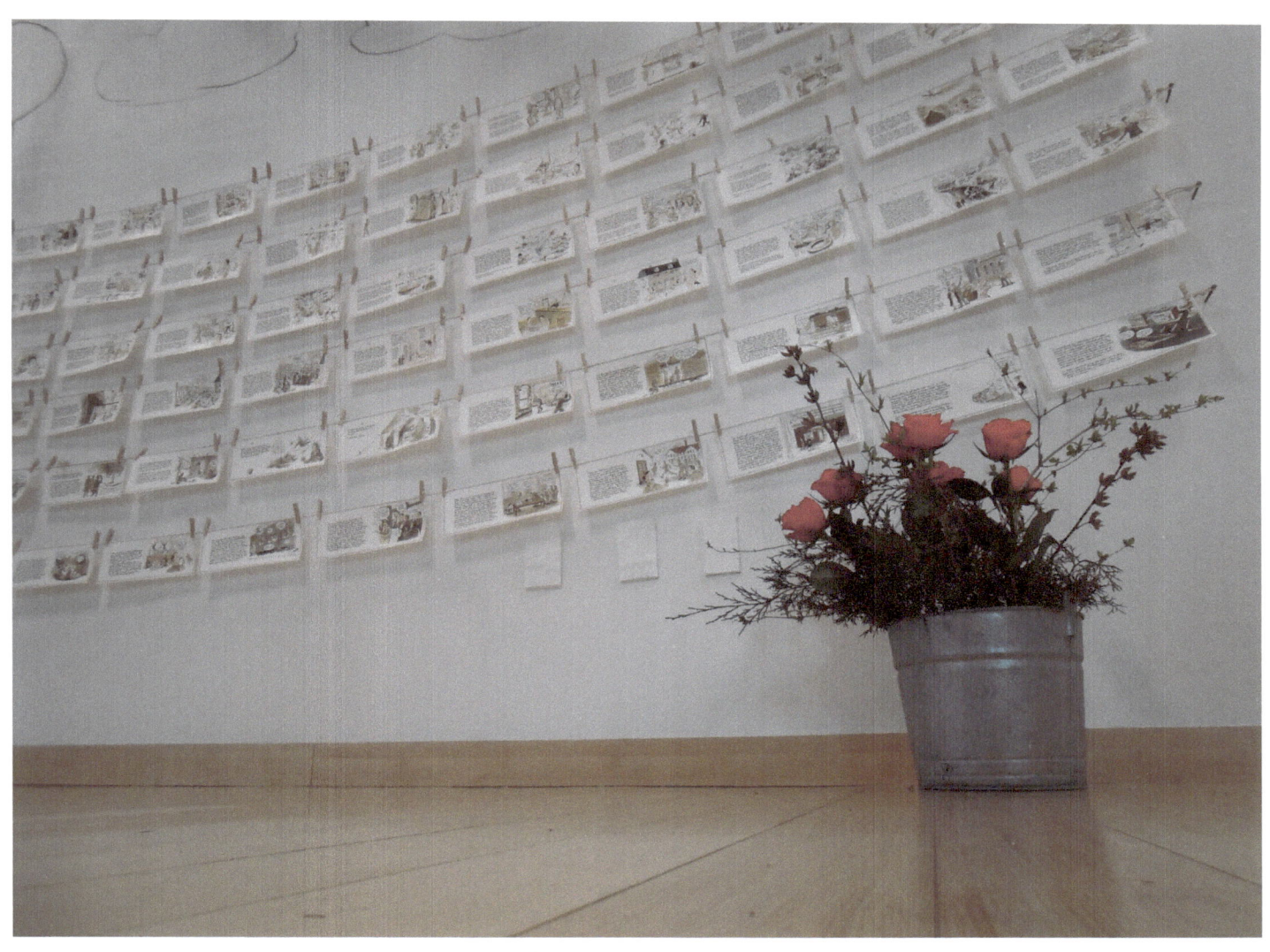

Pages and Process, 2016
The Philip M. Meyers, Jr. Memorial Gallery
Mixed media (pages in photo from *Military Story*), Dimensions vary

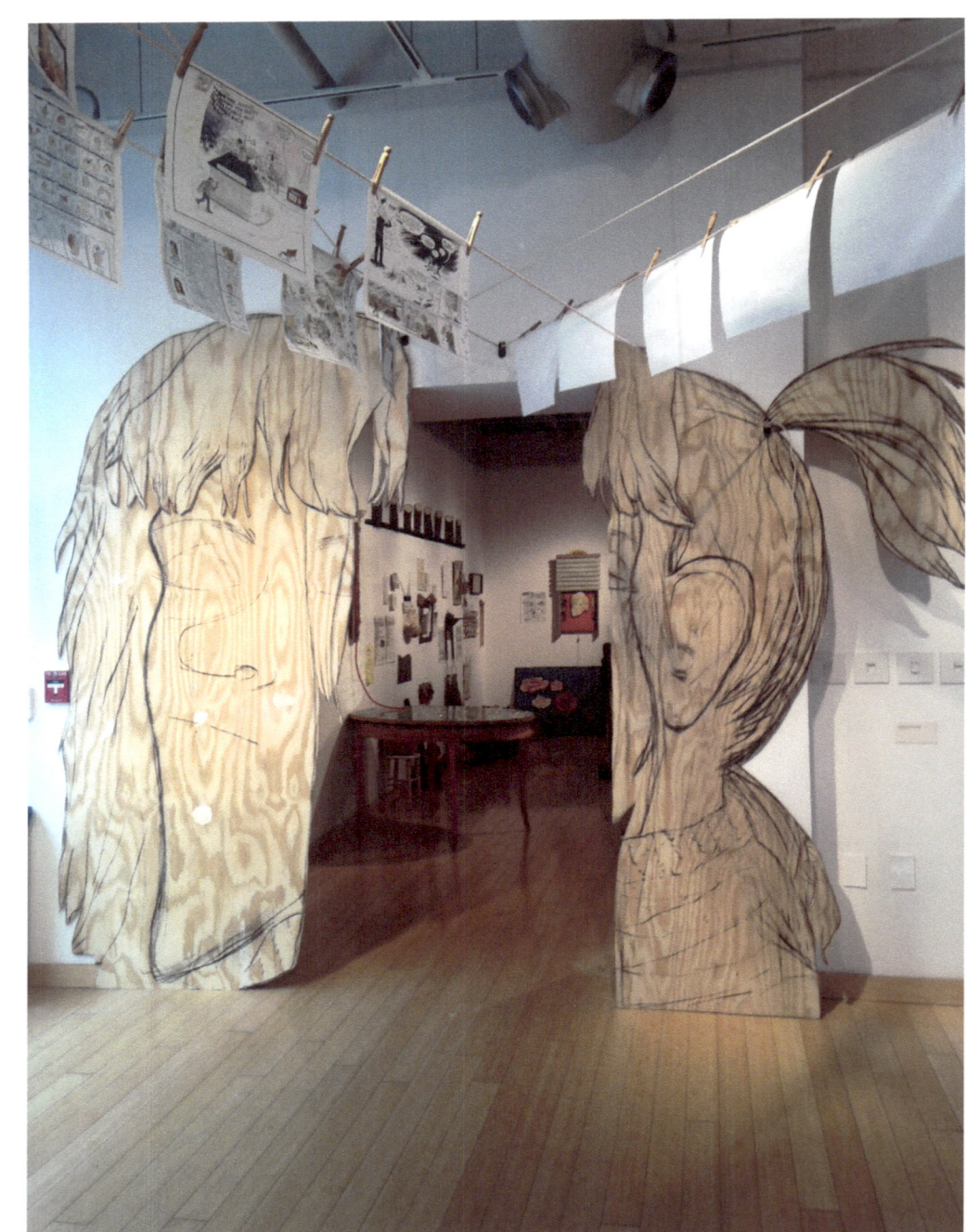

Pages and Process, 2016
The Philip M. Meyers, Jr. Memorial Gallery
Mixed media (pages in from *Portal into my Thinking*)

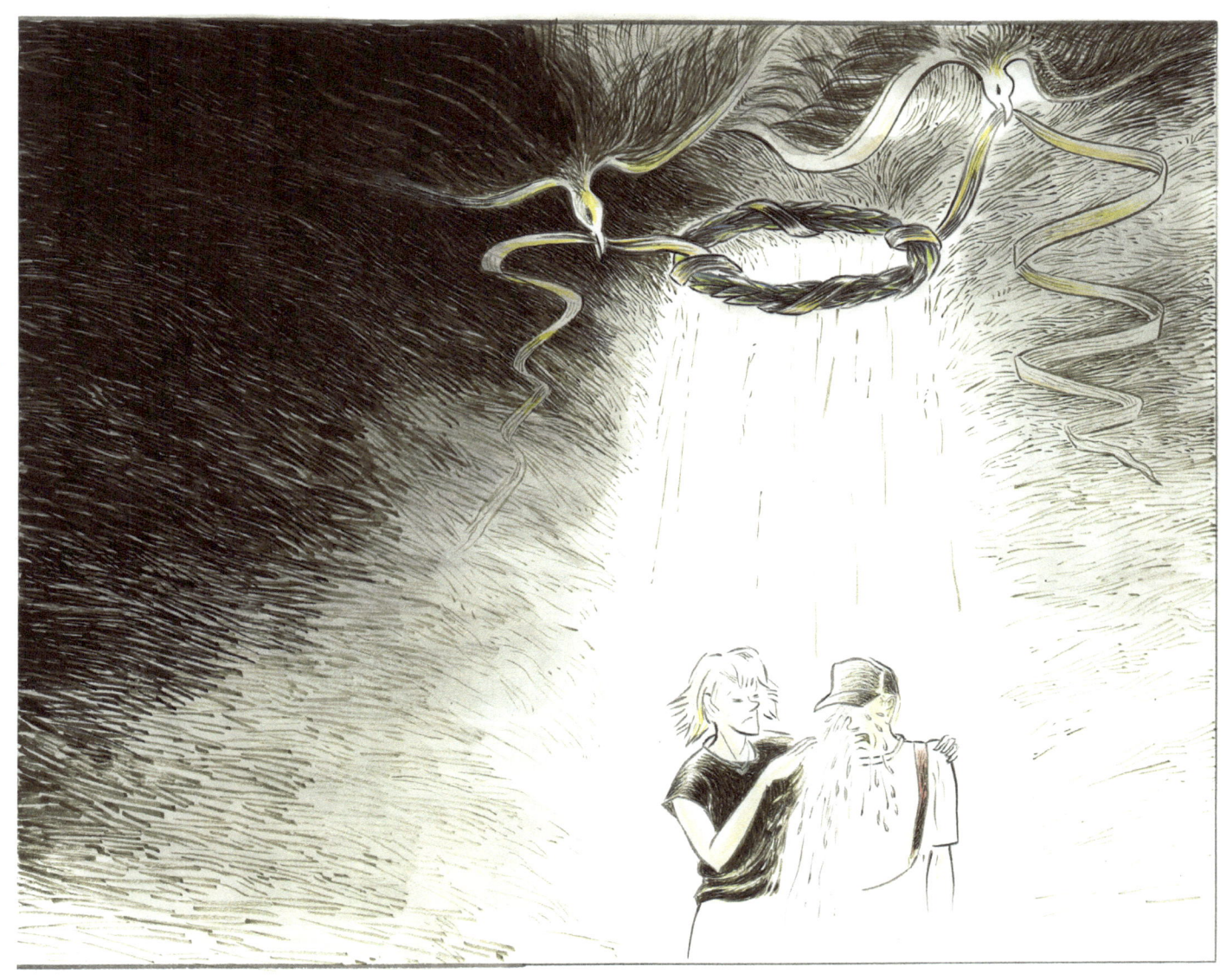

Soldier's Heart: The Campaign to Understand my WWII Veteran Father: A Daughter's Memoir, 2015
Fantagraphics Books, page 333

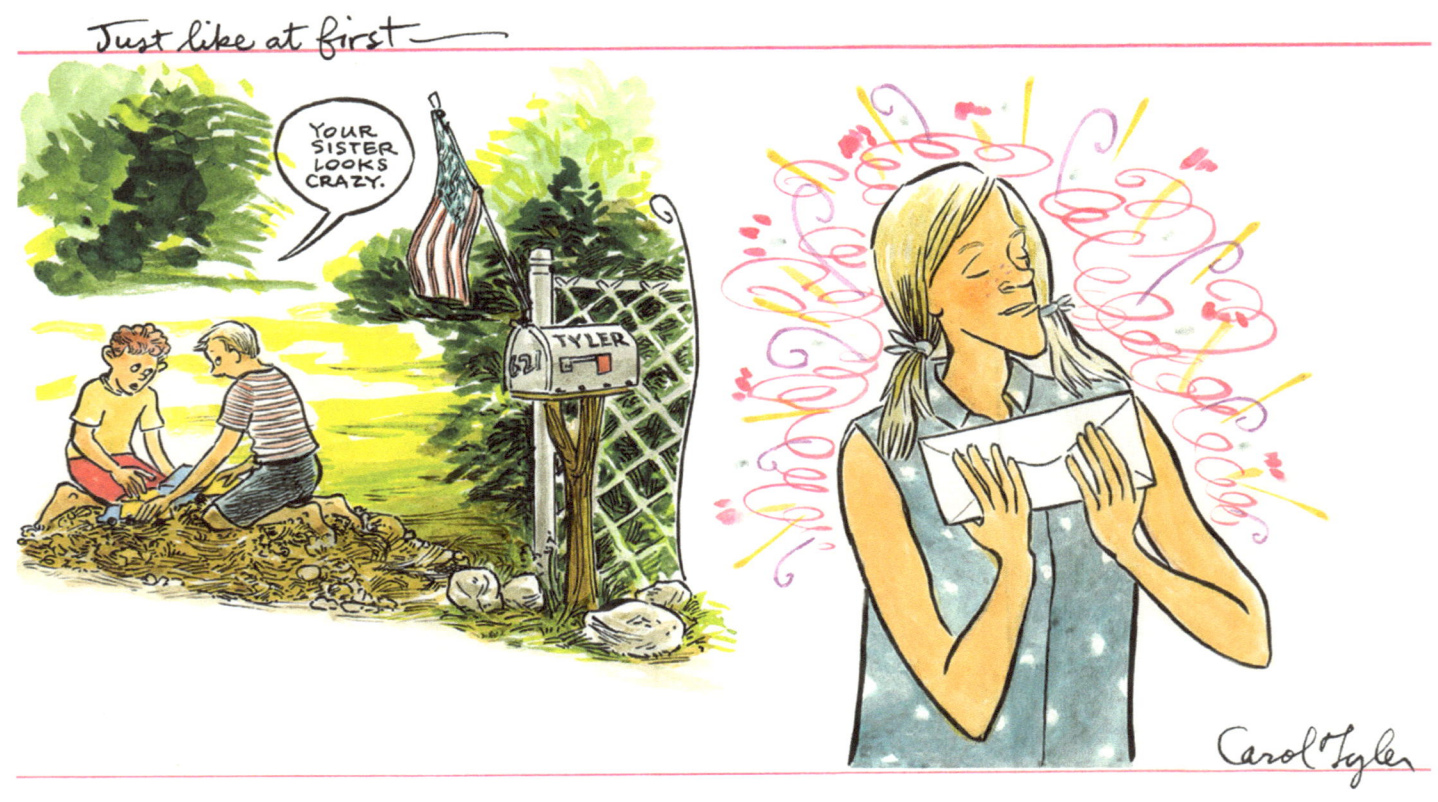

Fab4 MANIA, 2017
Fantagraphics Books, page 156

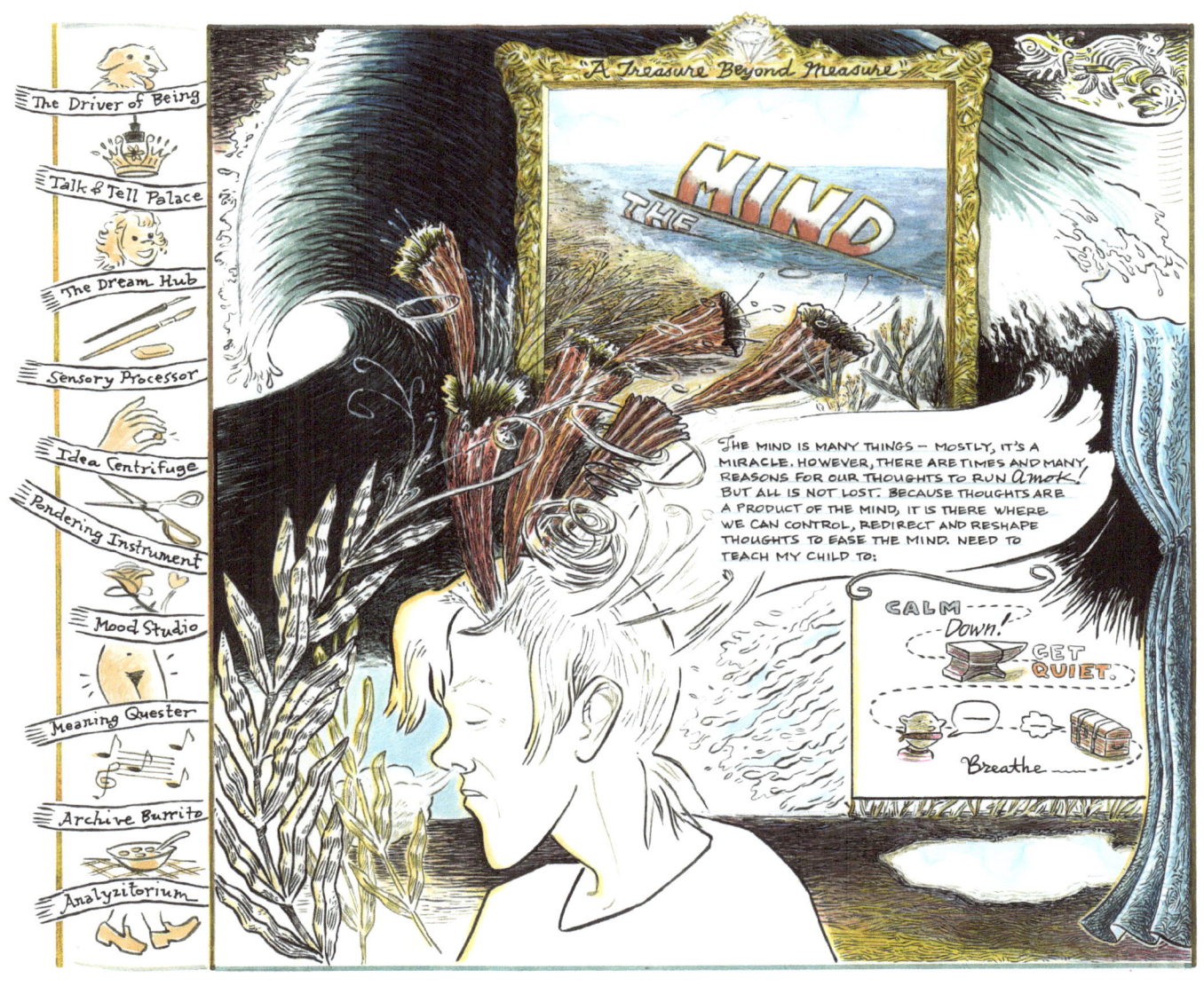

The Driver of Being

Talk & Tell Palace

The Dream Hub

Sensory Processor

Idea Centrifuge

Pondering Instrument

Mood Studio

Meaning Quester

Archive Burrito

Analyzitorium

"A Treasure Beyond Measure"

THE MIND

THE MIND IS MANY THINGS — MOSTLY, IT'S A MIRACLE. HOWEVER, THERE ARE TIMES AND MANY REASONS FOR OUR THOUGHTS TO RUN *amok!* BUT ALL IS NOT LOST. BECAUSE THOUGHTS ARE A PRODUCT OF THE MIND, IT IS THERE WHERE WE CAN CONTROL, REDIRECT AND RESHAPE THOUGHTS TO EASE THE MIND. NEED TO TEACH MY CHILD TO:

CALM Down! GET QUIET. Breathe

Soldier's Heart: The Campaign to Understand my WWII Veteran Father: A Daughter's Memoir, 2015
Fantagraphics Books, page 246

25

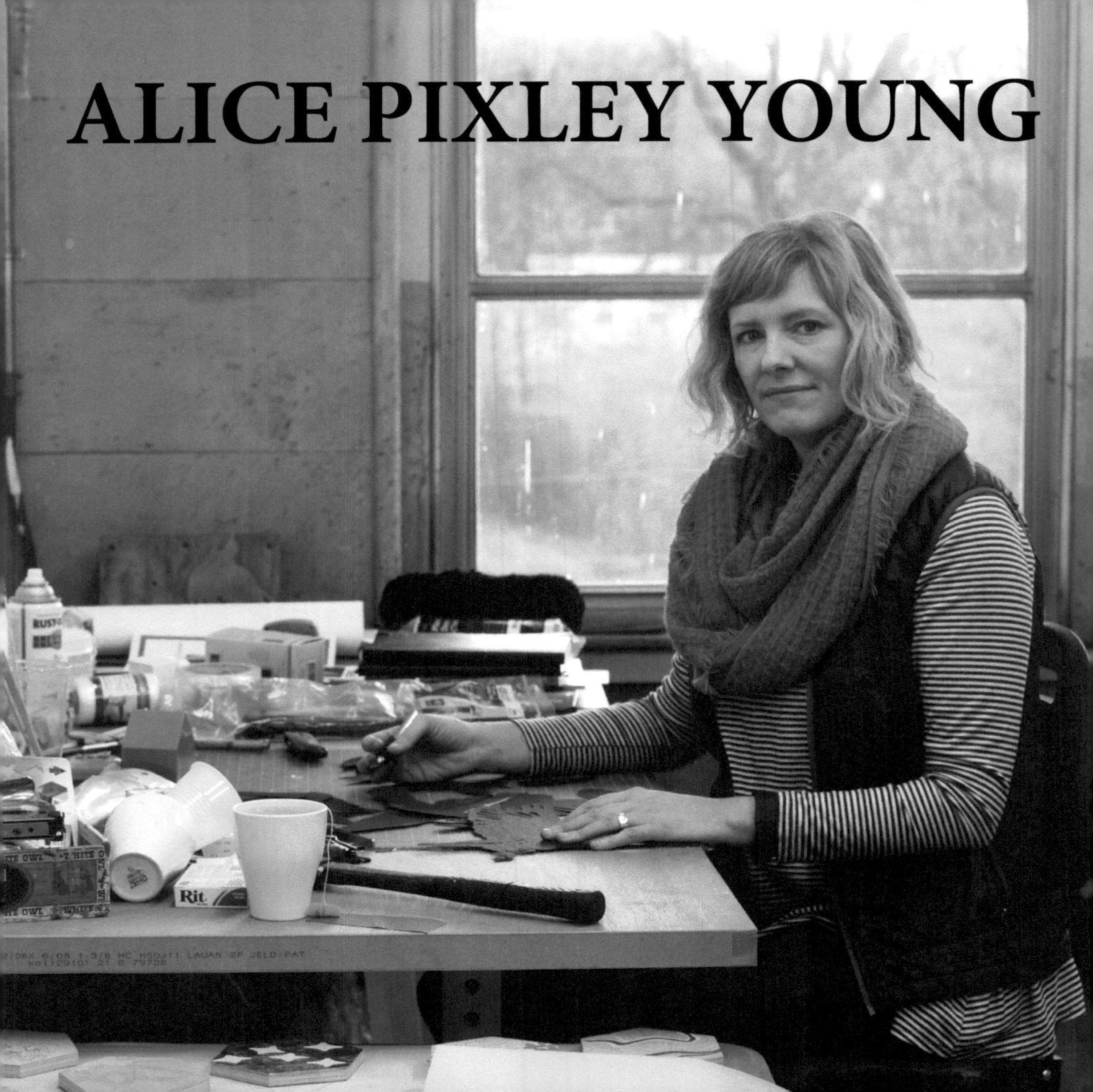

ALICE PIXLEY YOUNG

Alice Pixley Young describes Cincinnati not simply as her home, but as her artistic haven. To those puzzled why she wouldn't choose a more "metropolitan" city, Young praises Cincinnati's rustic beauty. She describes Cincinnati as "Beautiful...almost Manchester, England...kind of 19th century." Cincinnati's Music Hall, classic warehouses and old factories are imbued with a history that translates directly to Young's installation art. This beauty beneath the superficial is something that attracts Young.

Born in Washington, D.C., Alice Pixley Young grew up in the city's free museums. Her parents, both government workers, wholeheartedly supported her artistic passion. Young moved to Florida and earned a BFA in Printmaking and Painting from Ringling College of Art and Design. Young loved RCAD's smaller, more intimate program. As a senior she studied for a semester at the New York Studio Program, where she worked as an artist assistant to Michelle Stuart and in her own provided studio. This was an important experience as it gave her insight into a working artist's life and studio practice.

After taking a year off to work on a North Carolina farm, Young earned her MFA in Painting from the University of Maryland. Over the next few years, teaching jobs drew her to northern Pennsylvania and finally Cincinnati. From the very beginning of her tenure in Cincinnati, Young has taught at the School for Creative and Performing Arts, the University of Cincinnati and Northern Kentucky University. Early on she completed a master's in Art Education from the Art Academy of Cincinnati.

Her committed studio practice is a daily focus of her creative energy. Her active studio life has been a wellspring for her role as a teacher and mentor to her art students. Her work, which has grown from representational painting and drawing into multi-media installations, has won her national awards and accolades.

The spirit of challenge informs Young's art. She once worked entirely in black and white for a year. When her representational painting became almost too literal, Young turned to multimedia. Over the years, she has been awarded multiple residencies across the country. A grant from New York's Surdna Foundation allowed her to take a workshop in glass at Pilchuck Glass School where she learned mold making and glass casting, adding another layer to her work and studio practice. Young wants her installations to be evocative experiences transforming the walls of the gallery into an entirely new space.

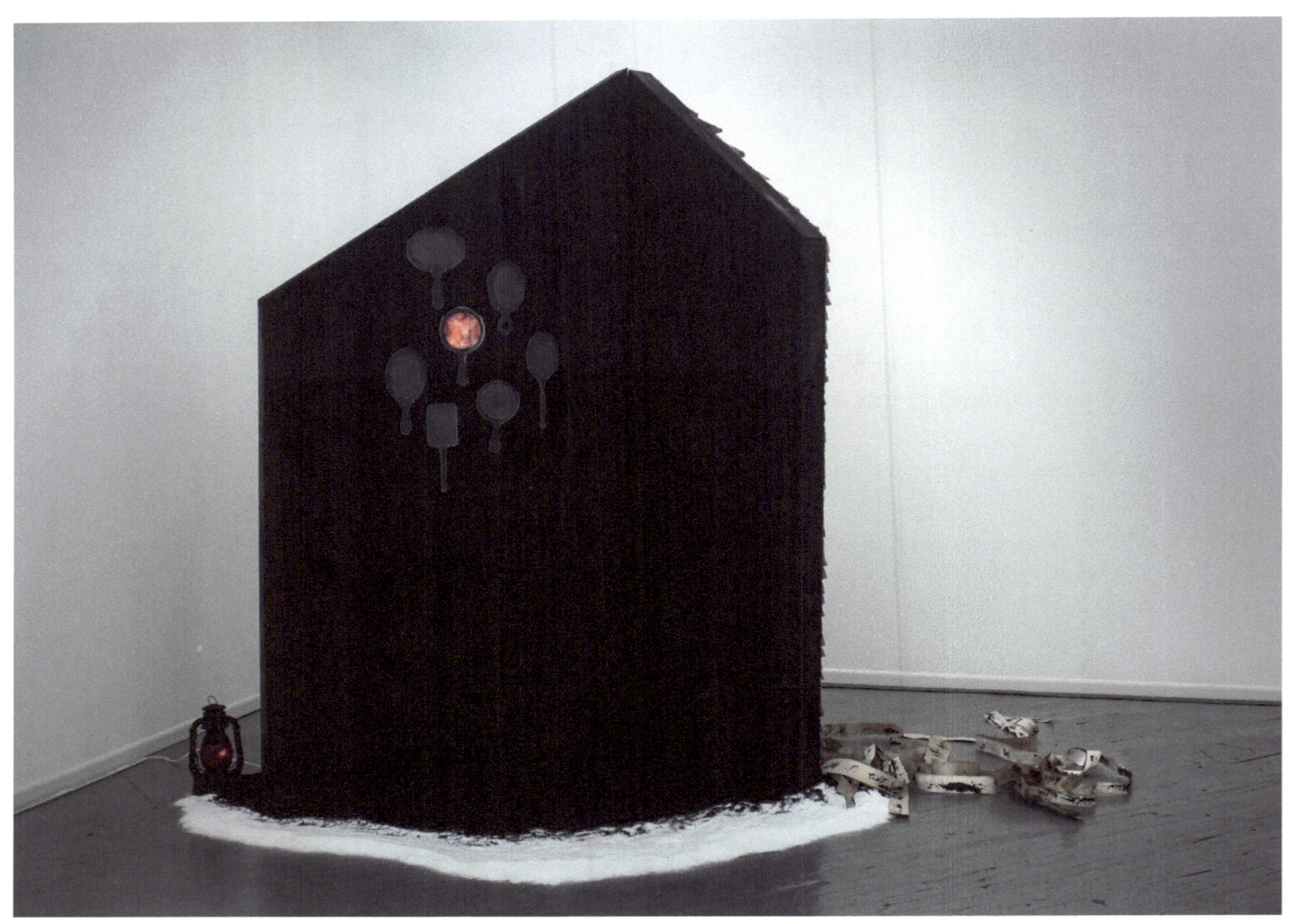

You Can't Go Home Again (detail), 2013
Kiln cast glass, video, graphite, coal, salt, dyed paper, ink, wood, found objects, 8' x 6' x 3'

An Interview with Alice

Emily Moores (EM): Did your content change as you transitioned into creating installations?

Alice Pixley Young (AY): My content has always been very focused on gender and the aesthetic of handiwork, but I think that it has evolved a lot into my biggest theme: the psychology of spaces (whether those are domestic interiors or landscapes). I think that we mythologize and place a lot of personal baggage onto those spaces. So anything from horror to fairy tale, that sort of sublime unreachable beauty is something that I like to explore in my work. I'm trying to tap into something that is not speakable.

EM: How does your use of domestic materials as a medium play into the content of your work?

AY: I am very interested in experimenting with things that I find that resonate with me. Resonate from a tactile or visual quality and also what they symbolize (culturally or historically). I have talked about using paper a lot, but I also use salts. I started using it a few years ago. I started using it like a body. Thinking about it being minerally based, but also all the fluids in our body that have a salty quality. Thinking about how that could be a representation. I have used roofing paper. It is interesting in the context that it is a membrane. It becomes one of the layers of protections. I love the deep dense blackness. It is really cuttable. It is also this super deluxe, dense black. I have used coal dust for the same reason. It also has that mineral quality, i.e., it is from the earth. There is the environmental connection, especially in this area, where we have so much coal mining.

EM: How do you decide on your content for each piece?

AY: I would love to say that I go into the studio with a clear idea of what I am going to make, but it is absolutely not like that. It is really pushing and pulling. Trying and experimenting. Reading about something and thinking that I have to try this material. Then either having a wonderful ah-ha moment, or, it is not going to work out, and I discard it. I am very much about material exploration. I see things at the big-box hardware stores, and I think 'I want that!' It is has nothing to do with what it is actually used for, but surely it will be great in an art piece. That is how I ended up with tar paper.

EM: Your materials help create your content.

AY: Yeah. It also doesn't hurt that I live with an architect. He started off as an artist. We are both very interested in the house as form, and the house as the materials that make it up, as materials that are useful to work with.

EM: Do you have any advice for people who are not familiar with installation in terms of figuring out how to decipher what a piece is about?

AY: I think that giving it time is really huge. Not dismissing offhand. Go in there and just be in the space. Think about the materials that are making it up and how it is sitting in the space. I don't know that it is so important for people to know all the time. I think it is important for people to have meaningful experiences, and you can't get that if you are in and out. It's all about giving yourself some time to be in a space and experience it.

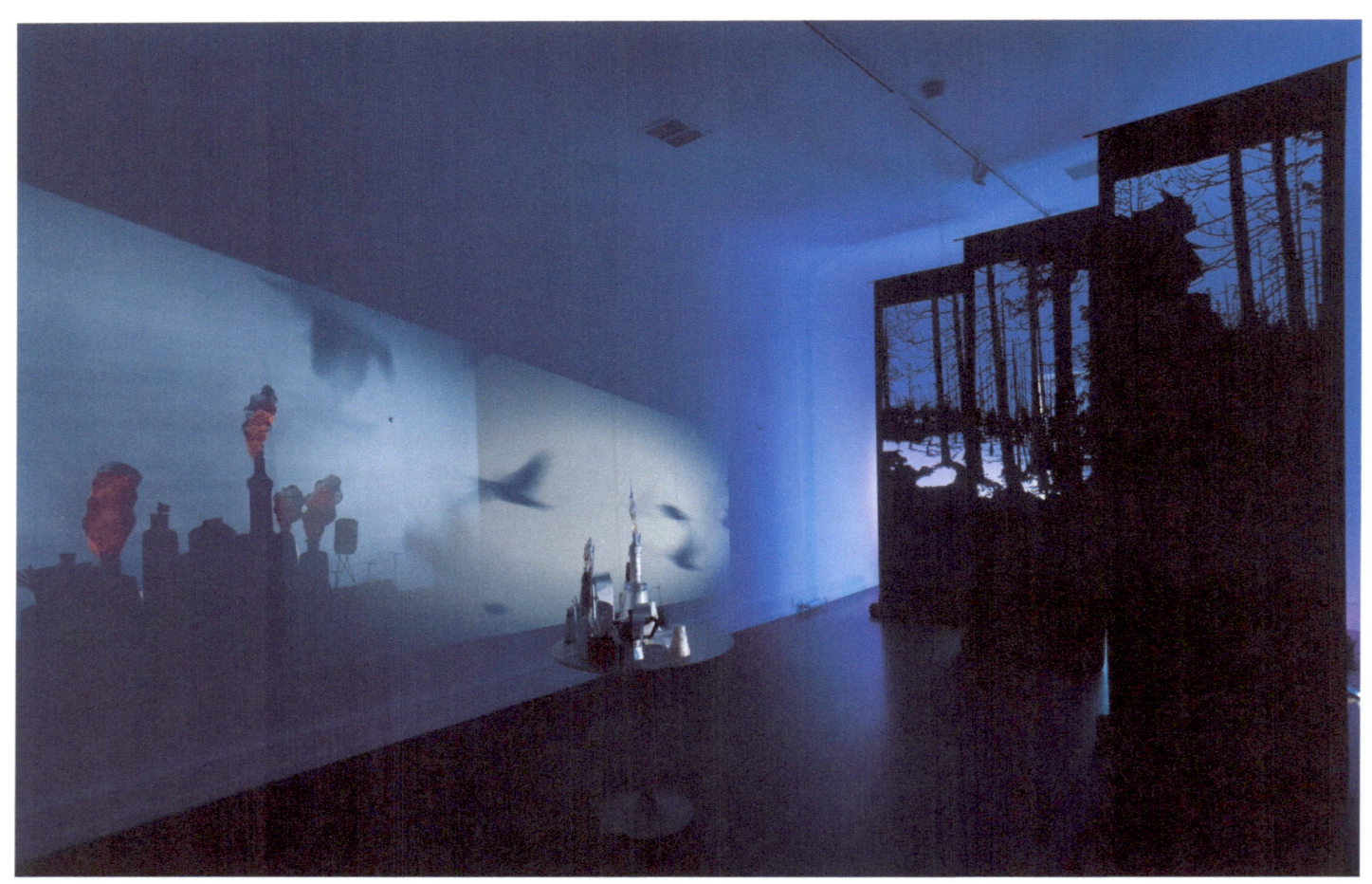

Geist (Left), 2016
Found objects, video, Dimensions vary

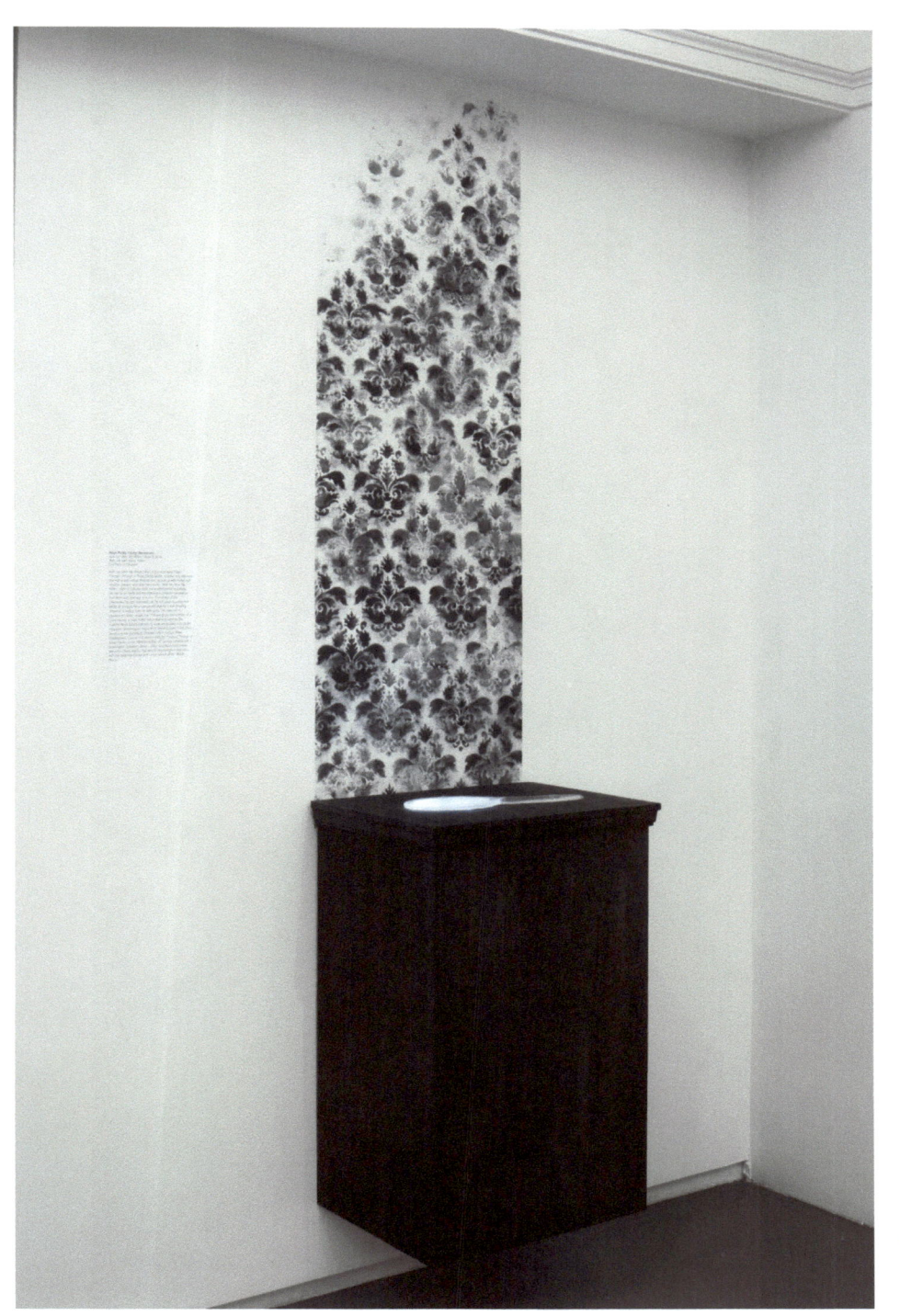

Will You Miss Me When I Burn, 2014
Ash, charcoal, kiln cast glass, video, wood, 96" x 24" x 15"

31

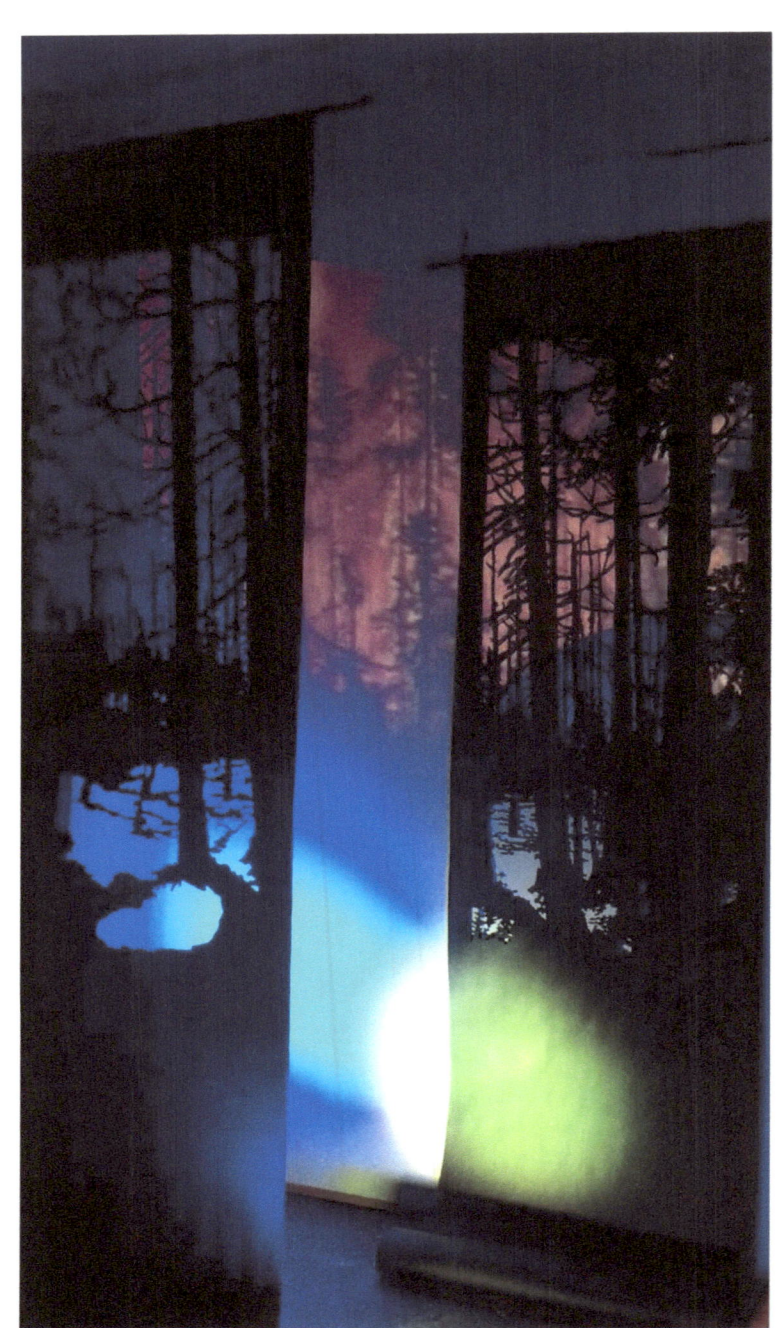

Sojourn, 2015
Roofing paper, video
projection, LED wall
washer lights, 10' x 15'
x 25'

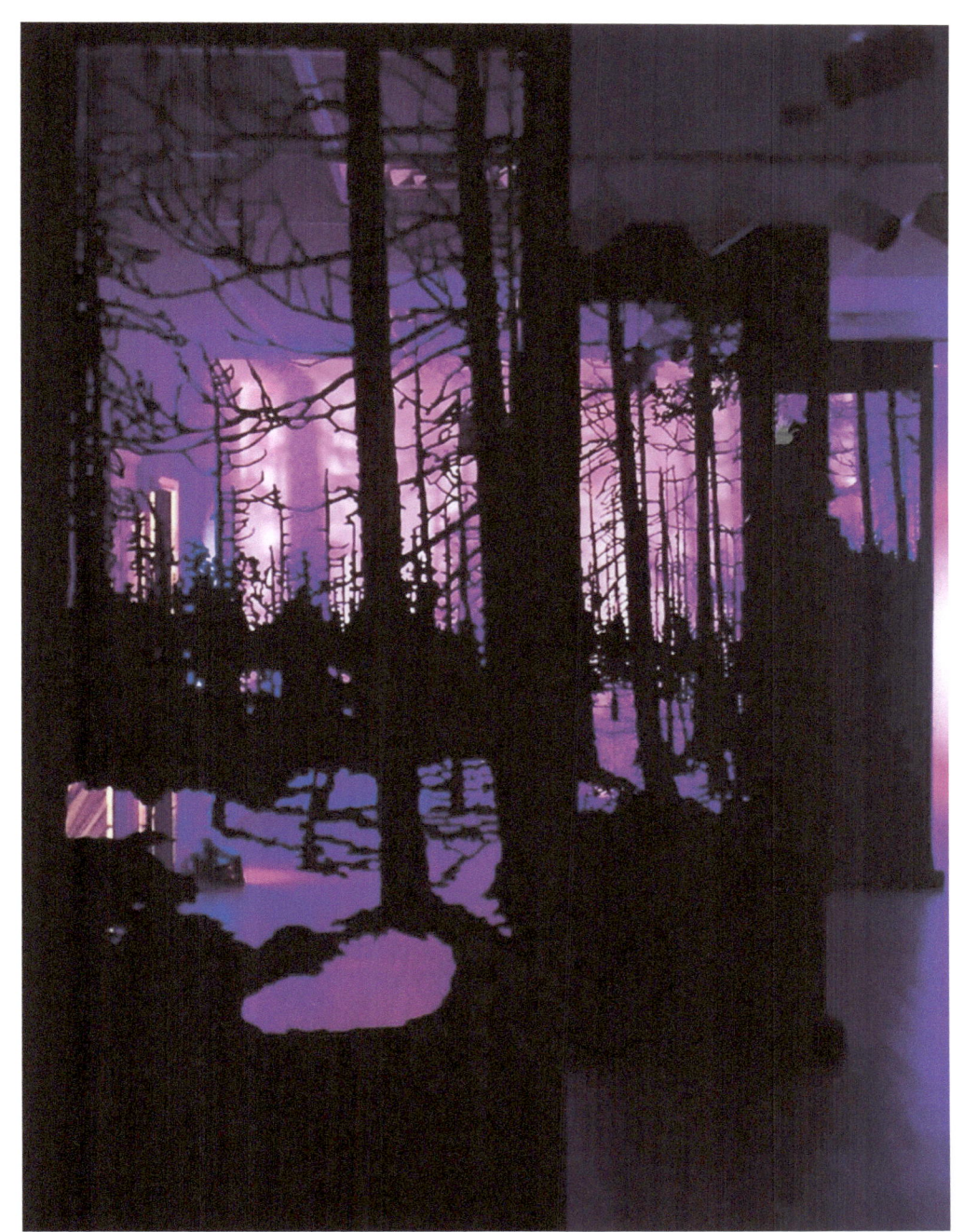

Sojourn (detail),
2015
Roofing paper, video
projection, LED wall
washer lights,
10' x 15' x 25'

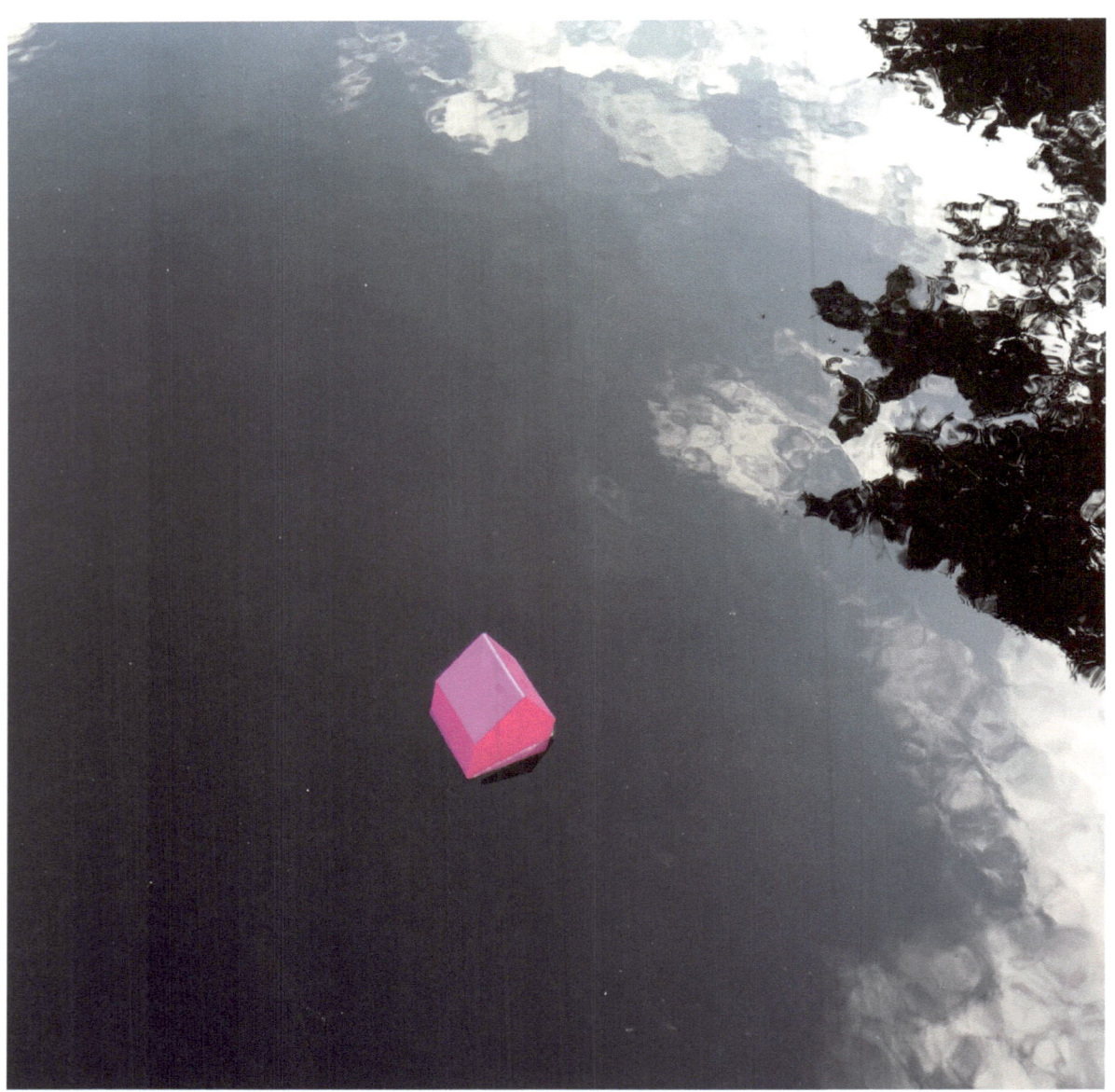

Lake House, 2016
Video still

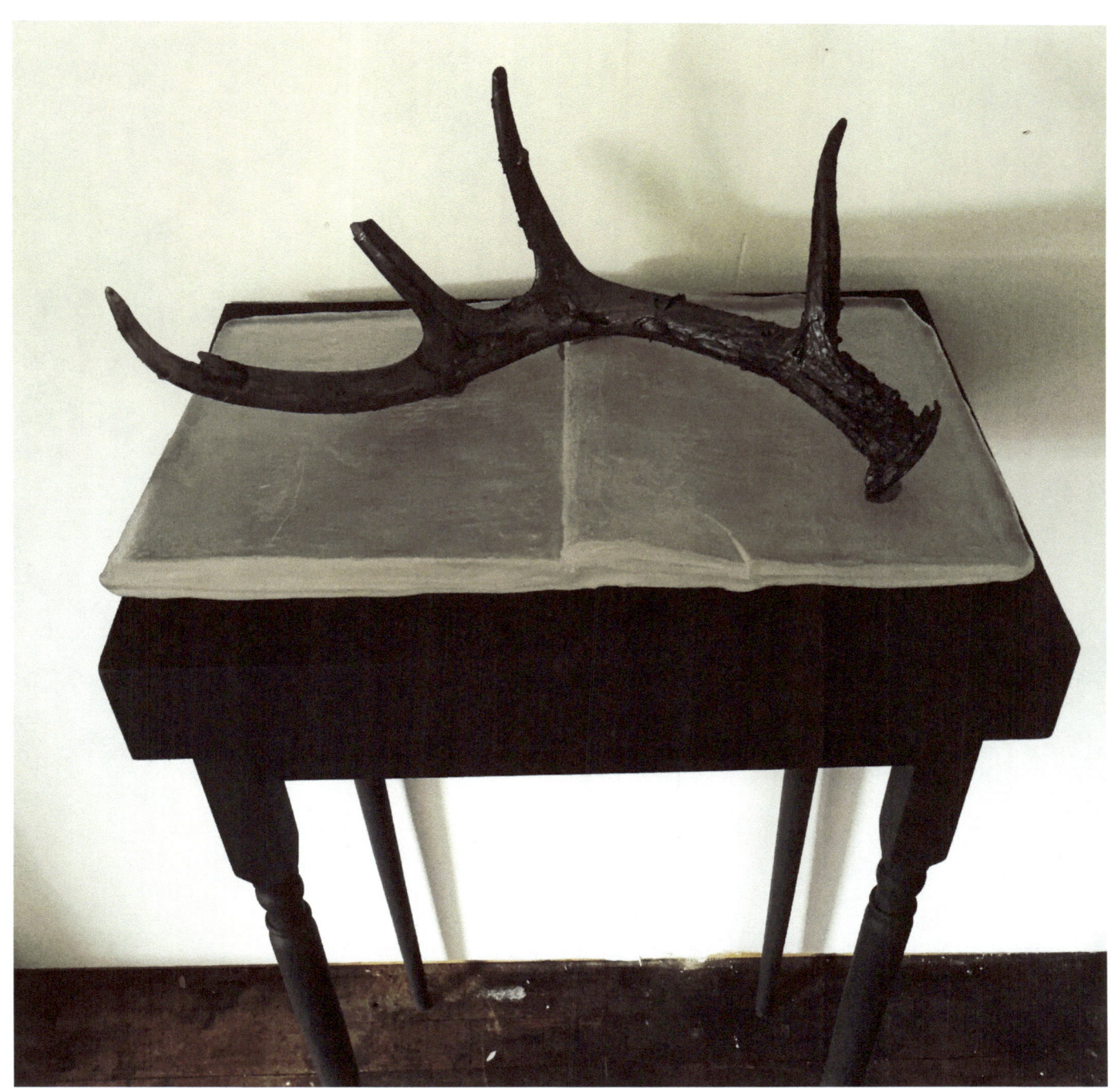

Glass Book, 2015
Kiln cast glass, pigments, 12" x 15" x 12"

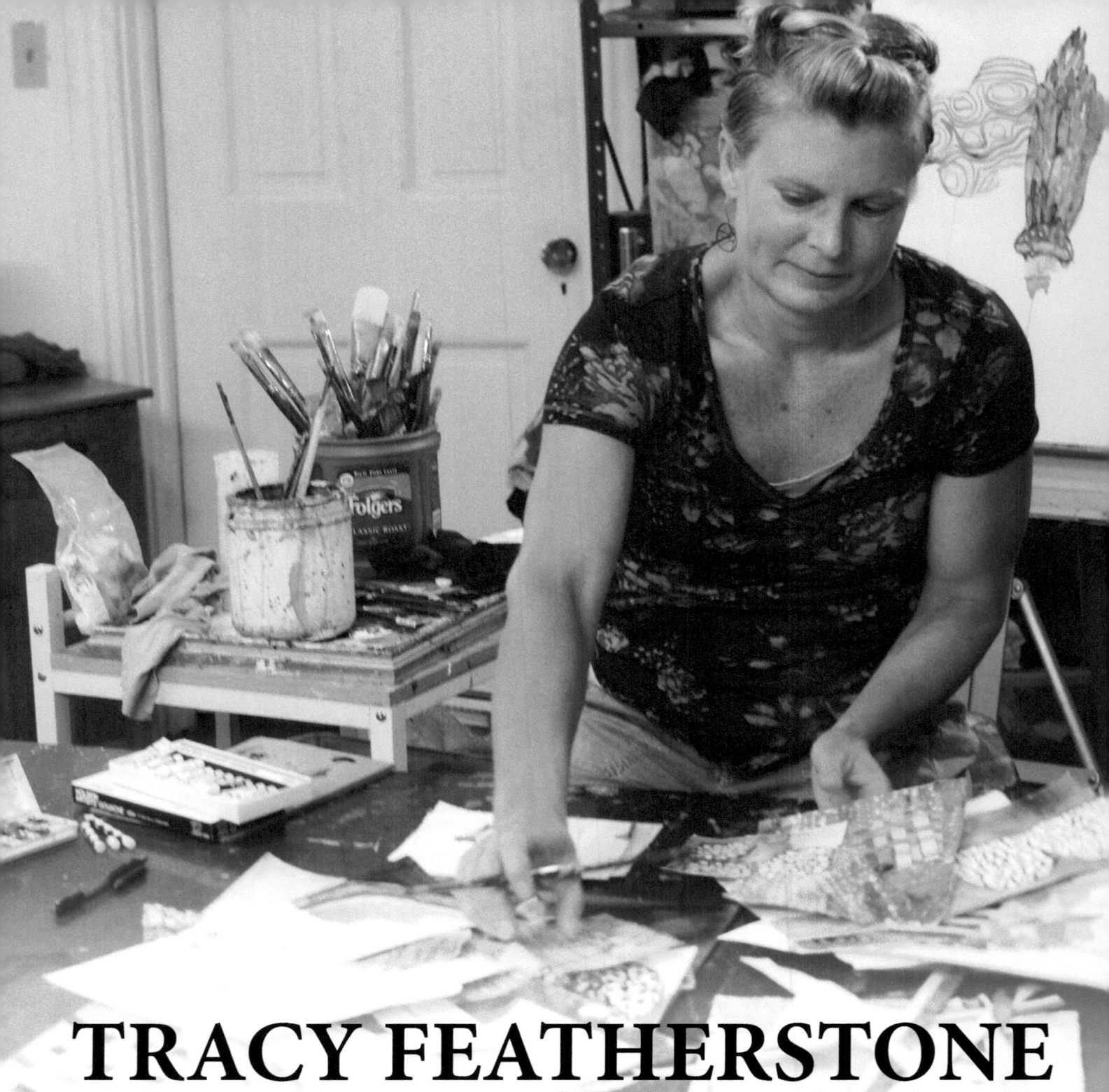

TRACY FEATHERSTONE

Tracy Featherstone is Cincinnati through and through. She graduated from Anderson High School and the University of Cincinnati's School of Design, Architecture, Art and Planning. In 1997 she and her husband moved to an apartment above Schaeper's Pharmacy in Northside. Featherstone worked for St. Teresa's Textile, near 1305 Gallery, and two years for ArtWorks before departing to receive her MFA in Printmaking from the University of Arizona.

A temporary position as a visiting faculty member took Featherstone to Grand Rapids University in Michigan. However, southwest Ohio again came calling. After she sent out a number of applications, Miami University offered Featherstone a job as Foundations Coordinator. Working with and teaching students suit her well. The intro-level courses provide students a solid foundation in design and idea-execution across a variety of formats. Additionally, the cross-discipline format meshes perfectly into Featherstone's own art. Featherstone has always strived toward the physical and immediate in her art. This first meant an attraction to drawing. Drawings are instant, able to be touched. Everyone can draw. The term "drawing" also encompasses a wide area. A "drawing" can be made by dragging ones feet across the grass. Who hasn't "drawn" in fresh snow?

Featherstone's graduate work saw an expansion from drawing to printmaking. She views her experience in printmaking as an evolutionary step from her drawing toward the environmental and sculptural work she produces today. However, Featherstone often felt the printmaking process to be frustrating and slow. She found more joy in creating the printing plates than in producing the actual prints.

Featherstone's work with the students at Miami University has pushed her art into exciting new mediums. Her position requires her to work with both first years and graduate students. Inspired by her graduate students, she branched into ceramics. The complexity of ceramics required a degree of humility Featherstone was glad to experience. She learned under Dennis Tobin, side-by-side with undergraduate students.

Though initially intimidated by having a Professor of Art in their ceramics class, Featherstone says the undergrads' nerves flew out the window once they saw how bad she was at throwing a wheel. The students quickly adopted her into the group. Ceramics requires tireless, hands-on work. Not only does she learn from the undergraduates around her, but Featherstone provides a concrete example to the undergrads who see their instructor striving to continually learn.

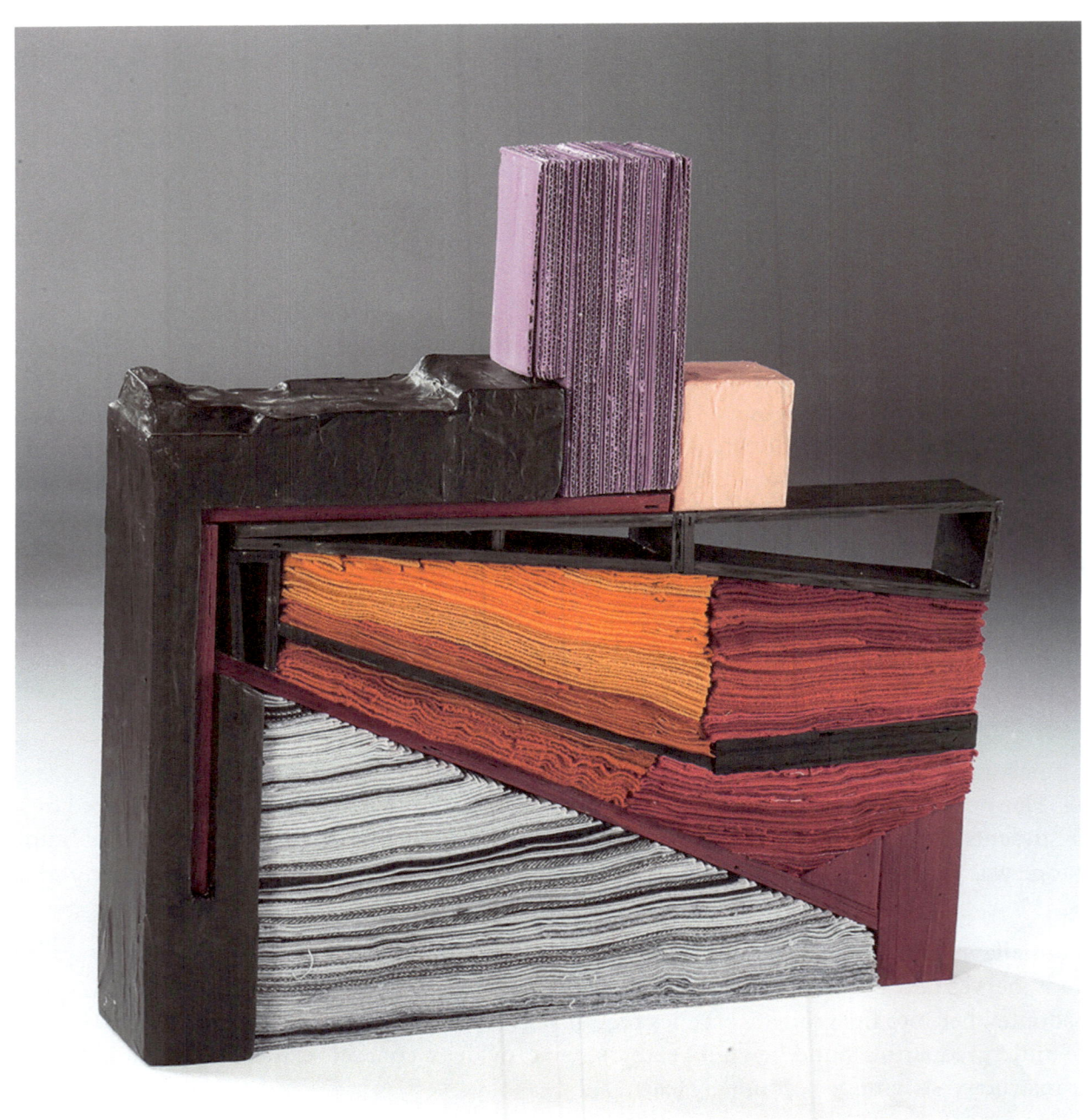

Amy Sillman Translated, 2013
Fabric, wood, paint, cardboard, 36" x 16" x 24"

An Interview with Tracy

Emily Moores (EM): Your art is very interactive. You have wearable pieces and use gold leaf to show interaction. Has that been a consistent theme in your work? Or did it arrive with sculpture?

Tracy Featherstone (TF): If I look back to when I was younger making artwork, I was always fascinated with artwork that shows the evidence of touch or the evidence of the process. In drawing, I was never really into clean, neat, super high-end drawings. It was super boring. I was into the kind of drawings that you could see the history of what happened to it. Sculpture is the same way.

With the wearable works, it is similar, but a little different. I was interested in actually using the body as a material. I was fascinated with this idea of could I change the hierarchy of the figure so could it become just like a piece of wood.

EM: Why is is the process or interaction important?

TF: Certainly vulnerability is important to me. I think this kind of rawness. This real human quality of being able to see the process and not hide it. I like the struggle. Whenever I see artwork like that I can feel it in my being. I can emote with that work of art. It is a way to connect to the viewer and emphathize with the viewer.

EM: You often play with negative space in your drawings. Is that something of interest to you, and does it transfer into your sculptures?

TF: I tend to be an artist that edits a lot rather than adds more. I like the idea of saying as much as you can with as little as possible. The drawings with negative space are a part of a series called 'In Mid Translation.' I took those from collages or different things that I made into Photoshop and erased a bunch of information. There were these little particles left. The 'In Mid Translation' summary is the inefficiency of communication. We always try to communicate, but you can never perfectly communicate. The parts of the drawing are the leftover fragments. The viewers can only see part of the picture and have to fill in the rest in their mind.

EM: Talk about your use of color. How do you decide what areas remain the color of the material?

TF: One of the reasons I specifically started using ceramics was that I wanted to use "dirt" as a material. So, showing the raw clay is an important part of the piece. On certain areas intense colors are poured or splashed on the clay pieces. This is inspired by many of the shrines I saw while traveling in India. As a way to pay homage to a particular deity, people would often bring colored powder or paint to the location and touch or splash the location with these materials. This can often be seen in alleyways, doorways, streets, etc. I loved the way bright colors (gaudy by American standards) were celebrated and existed simultaneously with other dirt and refuse around the location. The dirt and the glitz all became part of a magic concoction.

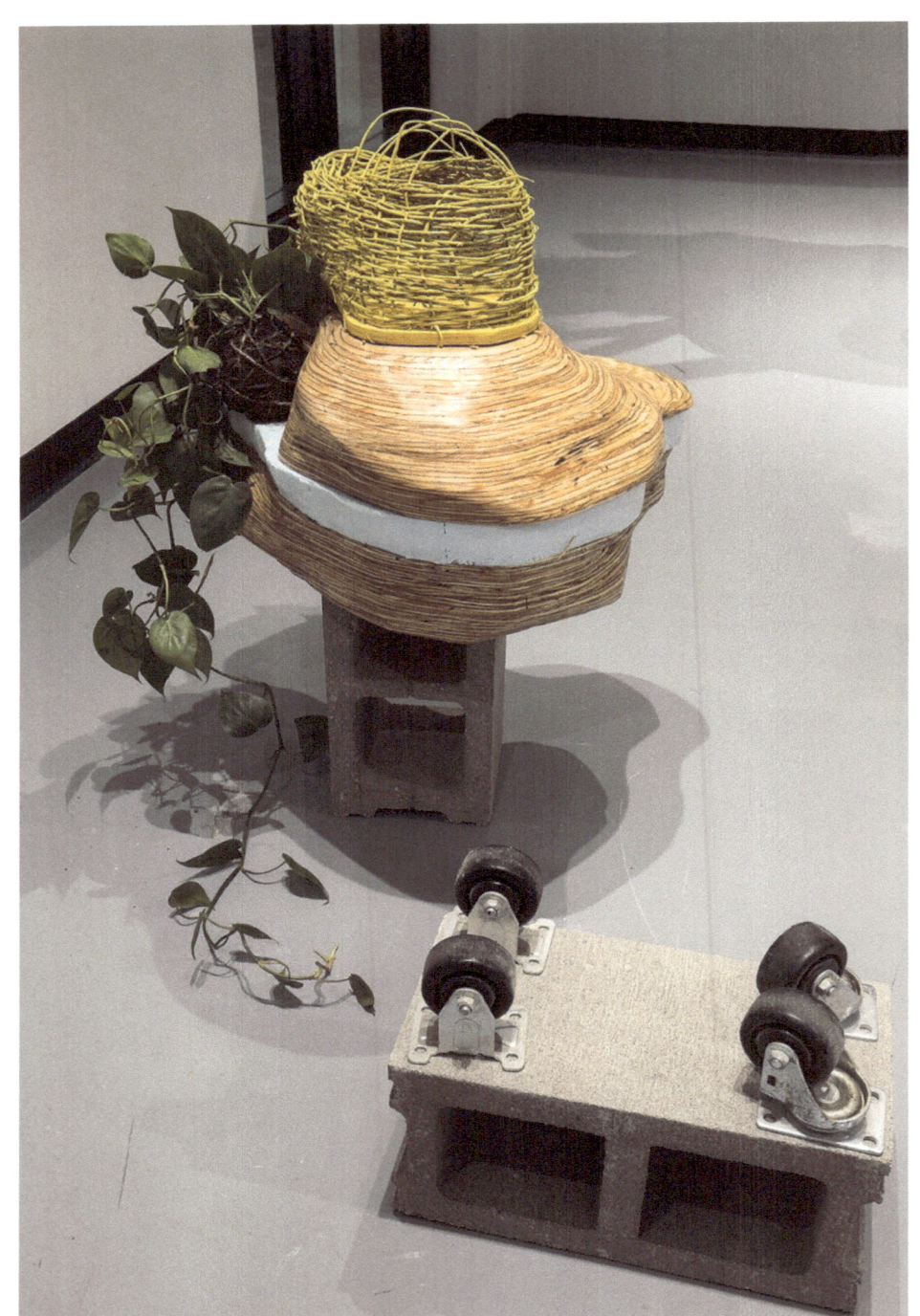

Hybrid Growth, 2016
Wood, foam, cement
block, wheels, plant,
woven vines, spray
paint, 33" x 36" x 13"

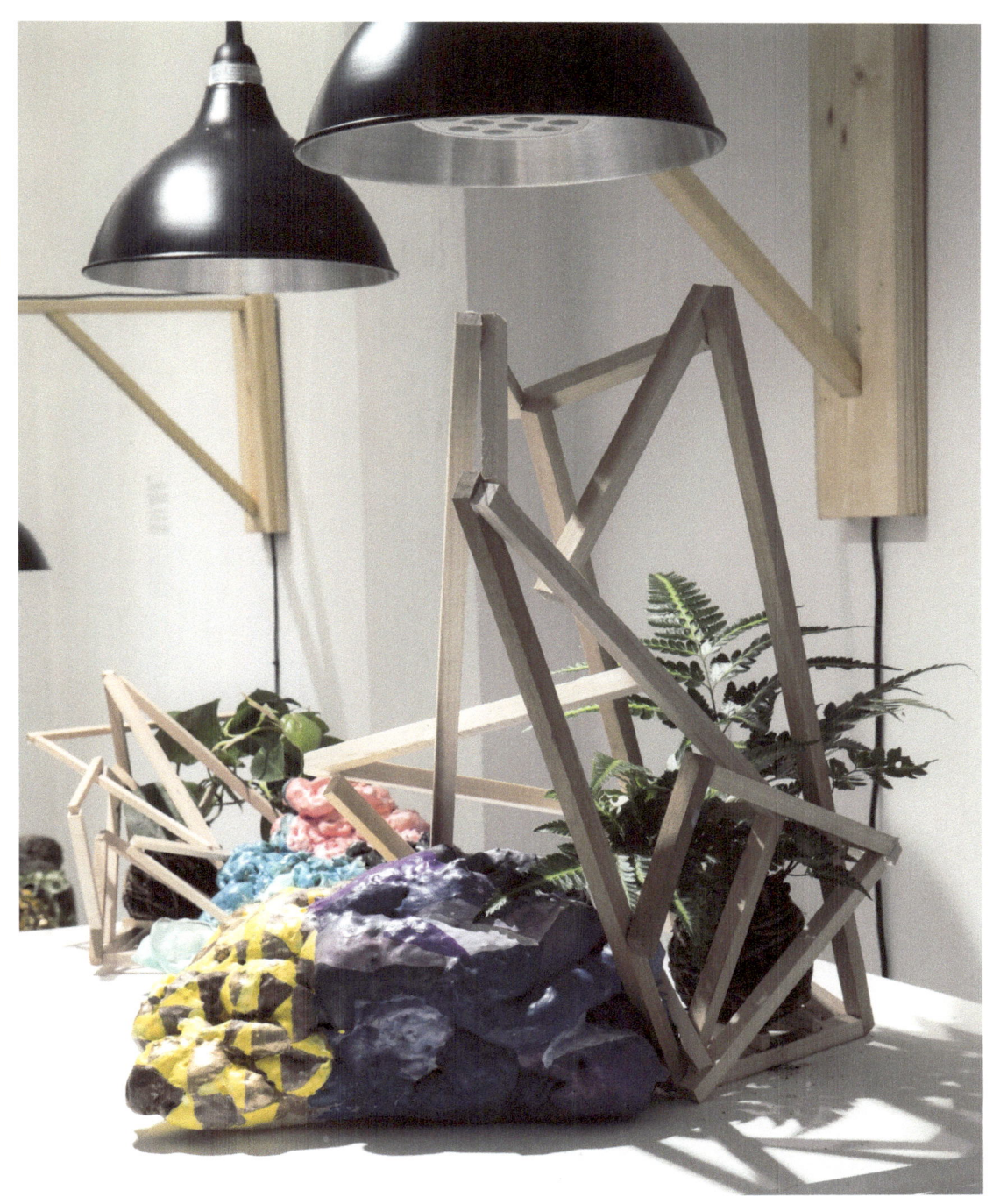

Diamonds and Mountains, 2016
Foam, wood, plant,
acrylic paint,
12" x 16" x 16"

41

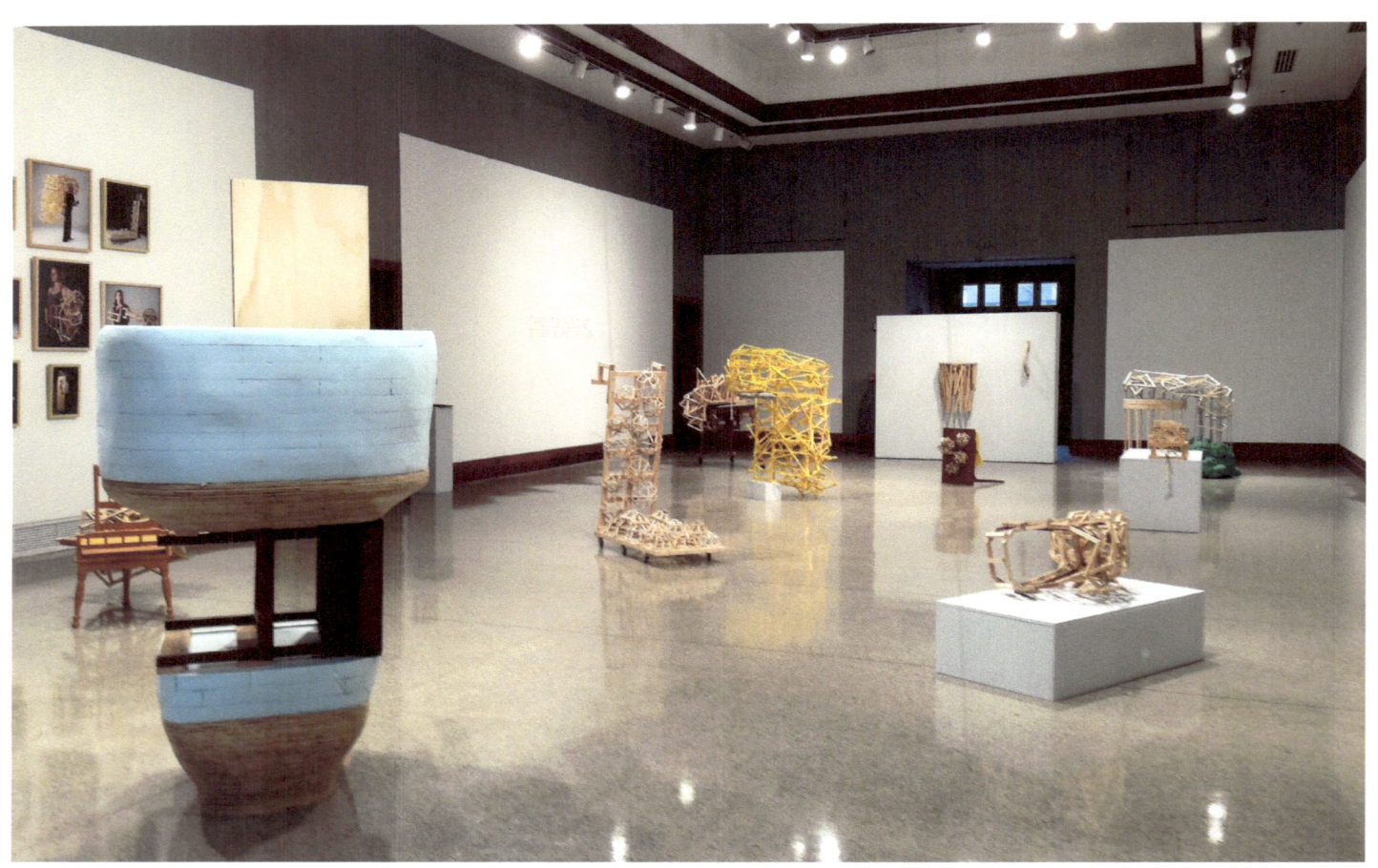

Between Me and the Floor, 2013
Georgetown College
Mixed media, Dimensions vary

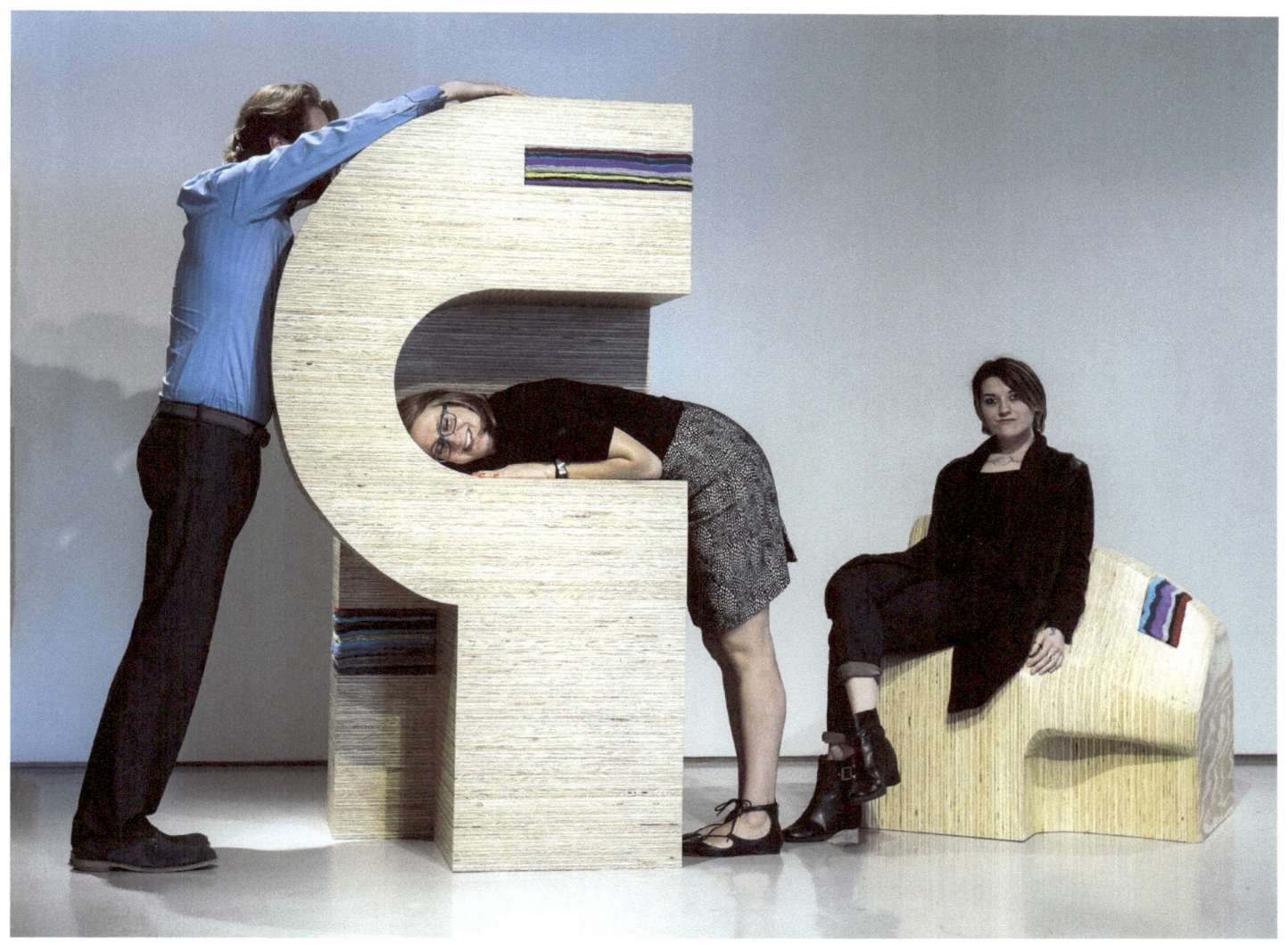

Passively Interactive Sculpture: Mounds, 2016
Wood, fabric, Dimensions vary

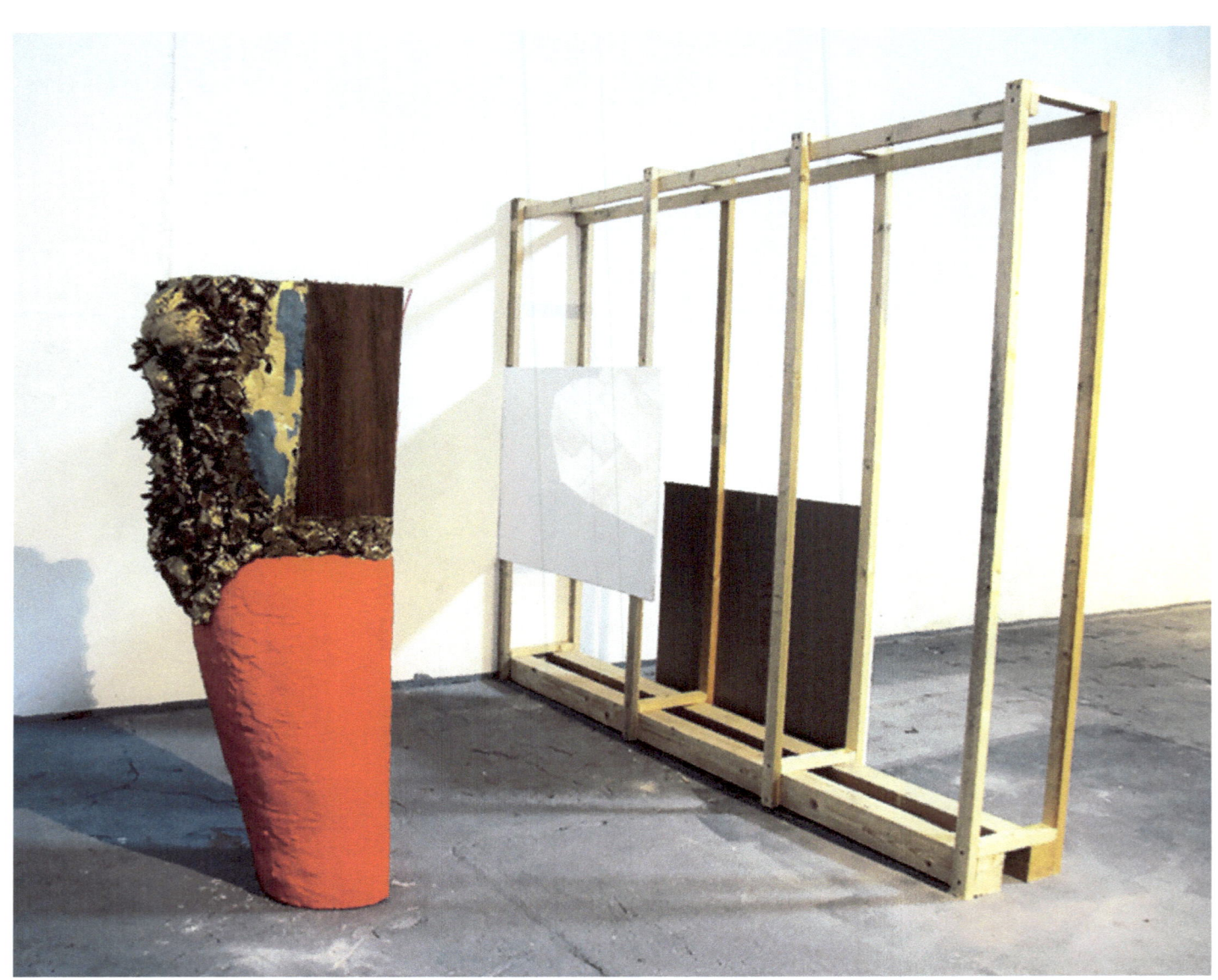

Orange Splat Translated, 2013
Wood, foam, plaster, paint, 30" x 60" x 30"

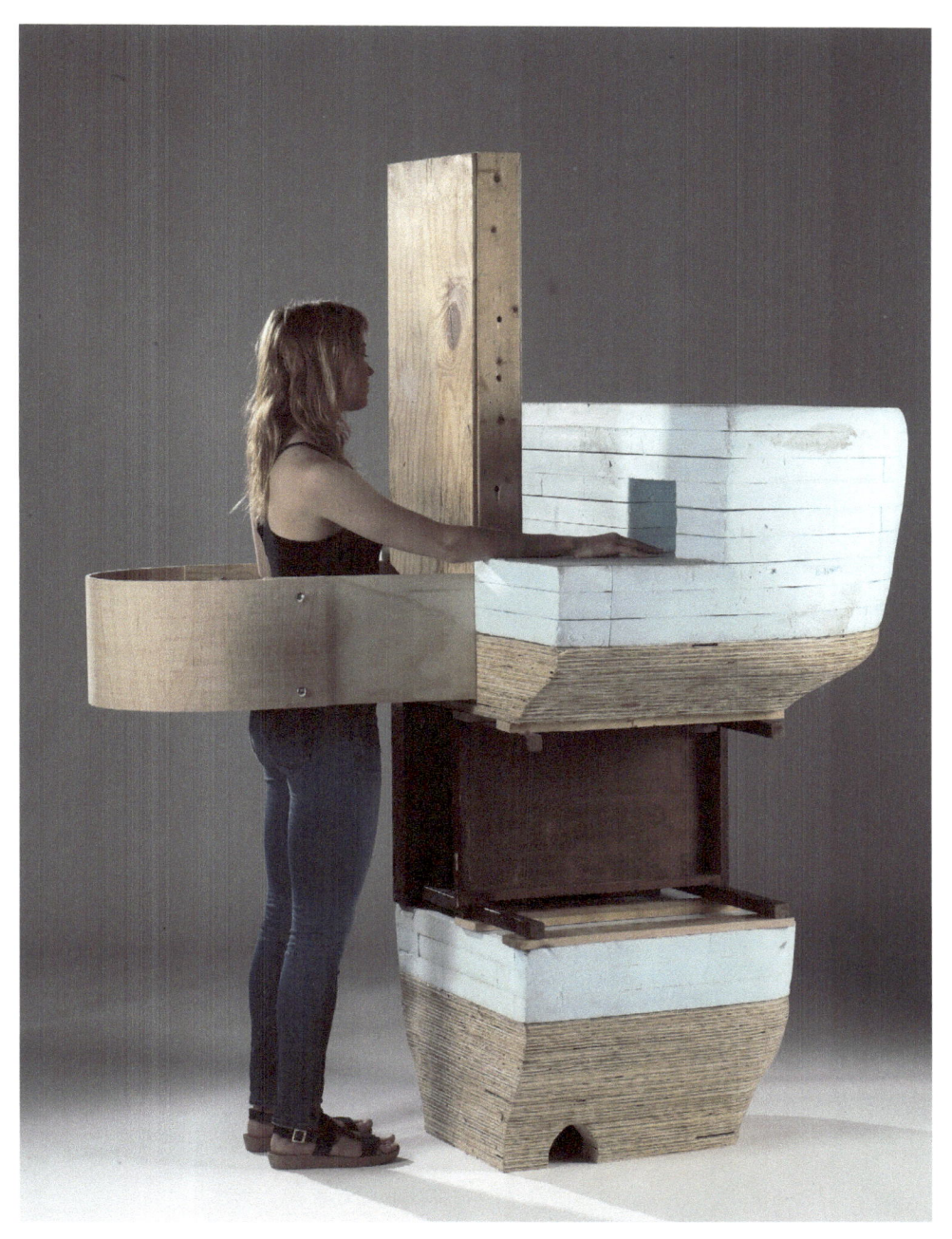

Passively Interactive Sculpture: Obstruction, 2013
Wood, table, foam, wallpaper,
40" x 34" x 84"

45

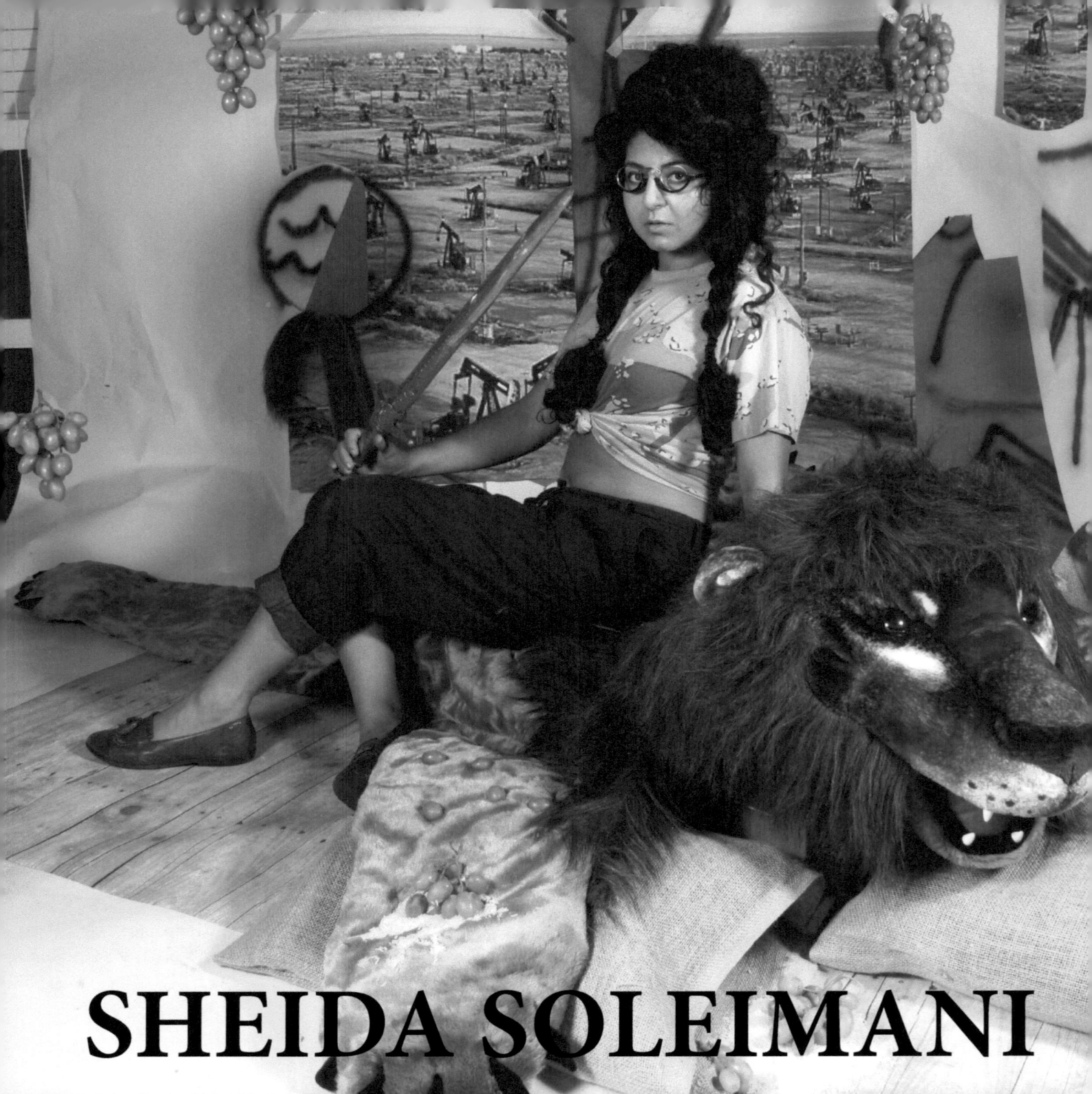

SHEIDA SOLEIMANI

Though Sheida Soleimani grew up in America's Midwest, Iran molds her art. Born to Iranian expatriates, Soleimani did not learn to speak English until she was six. Her parents worked to ensure Soleimani would remember her culture and heritage.

Soleimani's father, Manoocher Soleimani, was an activist in Iran after the fall of the Shah. He distributed flyers and organized rallies and marches. Patriotism made Manoocher a target, forcing him to escape Iran by horse. The government quickly arrested his wife. They tortured her for a year, trying to get to Manoocher. Unsuccessful, they released her. Shortly after, she escaped Iran with her ten-year-old daughter in a camel caravan, secreted under bags of rice.

Sheida Soleimani was born in Indianapolis, Indiana. Her father's work as a physician with UC Health relocated the family to Cincinnati. As a child, Soleimani was interested in art. Though not artists, her parents' creativity heavily influenced Soleimani. Her father discusses science as an art. Her mother worked as a wildlife restorator. Soleimani recalls spending countless hours cooking Persian food with her mother and talking revolution politics with her dad.

Soleimani grew up in Loveland and attended the University of Cincinnati's School of College of Design, Architecture, Art, and Planning (DAAP). College freed Soleimani to take risks. Her mother's work with animals kindled an interest in death that came to fruition in a darkroom photography class. A class assignment required Soleimani to explore personal narratives. Using herself as a stand-in for her imprisoned mother, Soleimani recreated and explored the Iranian prison cells.

After graduation, Soleimani took a year off. Working at Sidewinder Coffee near UC, however, Soleimani realized she required a challenge. She packed for Detroit and attended the Cranbrook Academy of Art. She loved the program. Cranbrook offers a radically different grad program: there are no professors. Four students study under one resident artist. Without assignments, Soleimani enjoyed unlimited studio time, where she began connecting her art to Iranian politics.

Inspired by her parents, Soleimani's art focuses on human rights. Her most recent work illuminates women tortured by the Iranian government. She takes images and information from friends and family in Iran and creates art focusing on those detained or murdered. Her work has caused Soleimani to be officially exiled from Iran. She has received death threats from neighborhood militias called the "Basij." In stark contrast, Soleimani's work has garnered her renown through the United States and beyond, and earned a litany of awards.

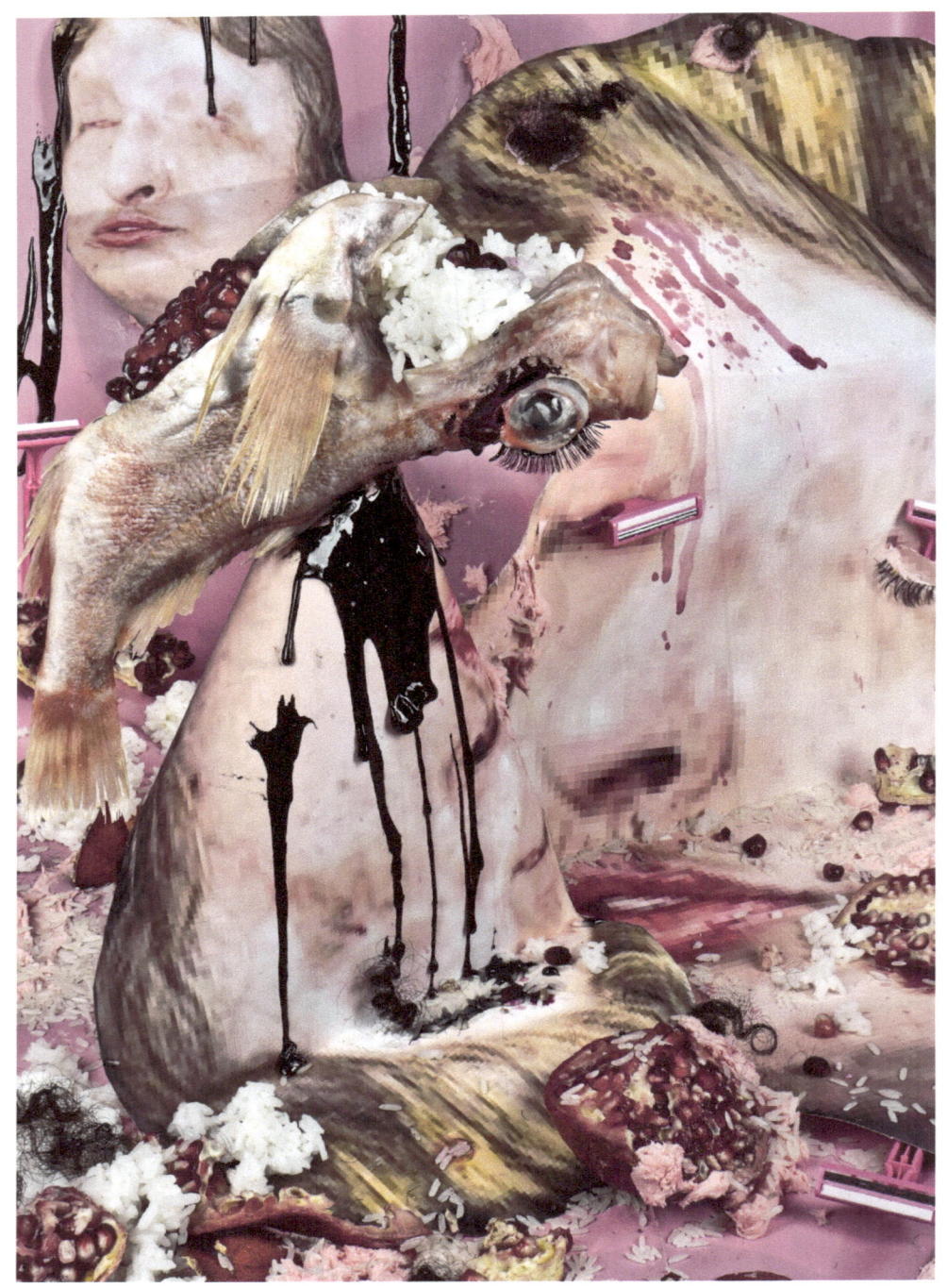

Filleting, 2015
Archival pigment print, 24" x 17"

An Interview with Sheida

Emily Moores (EM): Do your parents look at your art work? Do they like it?

Sheida Soleimani (SS):They help me with it a lot. When I was in grad school, I was doing this series where I was using my body and using myself. Using my body nude wearing a hijab. I wanted to [capture an image] on the beach when we were on vacation in Florida. I asked her [my mother] to help me take this picture. She was like, 'Are you going to be naked? Alright, don't tell your father I helped you.' We were on this resort beach, and she was handing me a towel every time someone walked by. She is really helpful with that. Or she will be like, "Sheida, I found a skull in the backyard today. Would you like to use it to think about death or is a skull too literal?" And my dad will be like, "A skull is too literal." They are my harshest critics. Is it so nice because they get all the content in my work.

EM: Your figures of stuffed women are specific people. Are you always talking about a specific person or do you talk about general political issues?

SS: I think both. The specific stories talk about what the larger political climate is. The images that I source, I will find them online from social media of people protesting. 'The National Anthem' was a lot about the general injustices towards people in the Iranian community. So, men were beaten for being found with their lovers that were men. Homosexuality is a crime punishable by law [in Iran]. That specific story would be the content for a piece, but that piece would be able to connect with all of the other pieces within the series.

Same thing with the women in the new series 'Into Oblivion.' Each image is a specific woman that has been executed by the Iranian government. Each story of each woman is different, but the general story is the same.

EM: Are all of these women activists? How does the government select the women?

SS: Seventy percent of them are falsely accused of drug trafficking charges. A lot of times they will have a male partner. The man will get caught and say, 'Actually, those drugs belong to my wife.' Then the government will go after the woman. There is so much blame put on women because they are the lesser sex. Reyhaneh Jabbari, the famous case, was executed for attacking her rapist. So she was raped, and she was trying to protect herself, and she attacked. He said that she attacked him. It doesn't matter that he was raping her.

EM: Are you in contact with the families?

SS: Some of them. There have been a few times where I have had images of their daughters or their sisters sent to me by family members. Sholeh Pakravan, who is Reyhaneh Jabbari's mother, sent me images and sometimes will post images of herself at her daughter's grave. So one of the images from 'Into Oblivion' is actually Sholeh Pakravan talking with her daughter on the phone one last time.

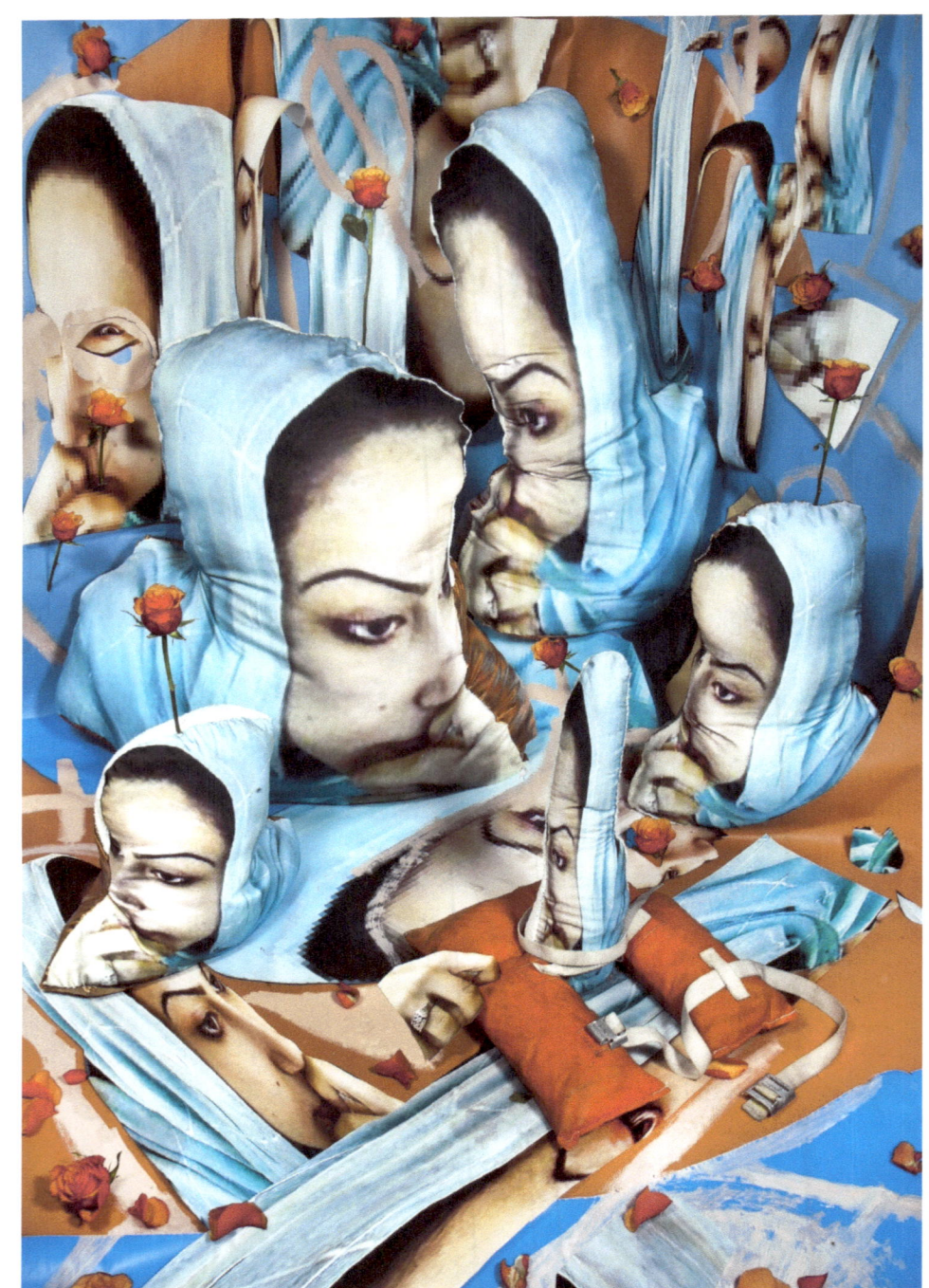

Delara, 2016
Archival pigment
print
40" x 27"

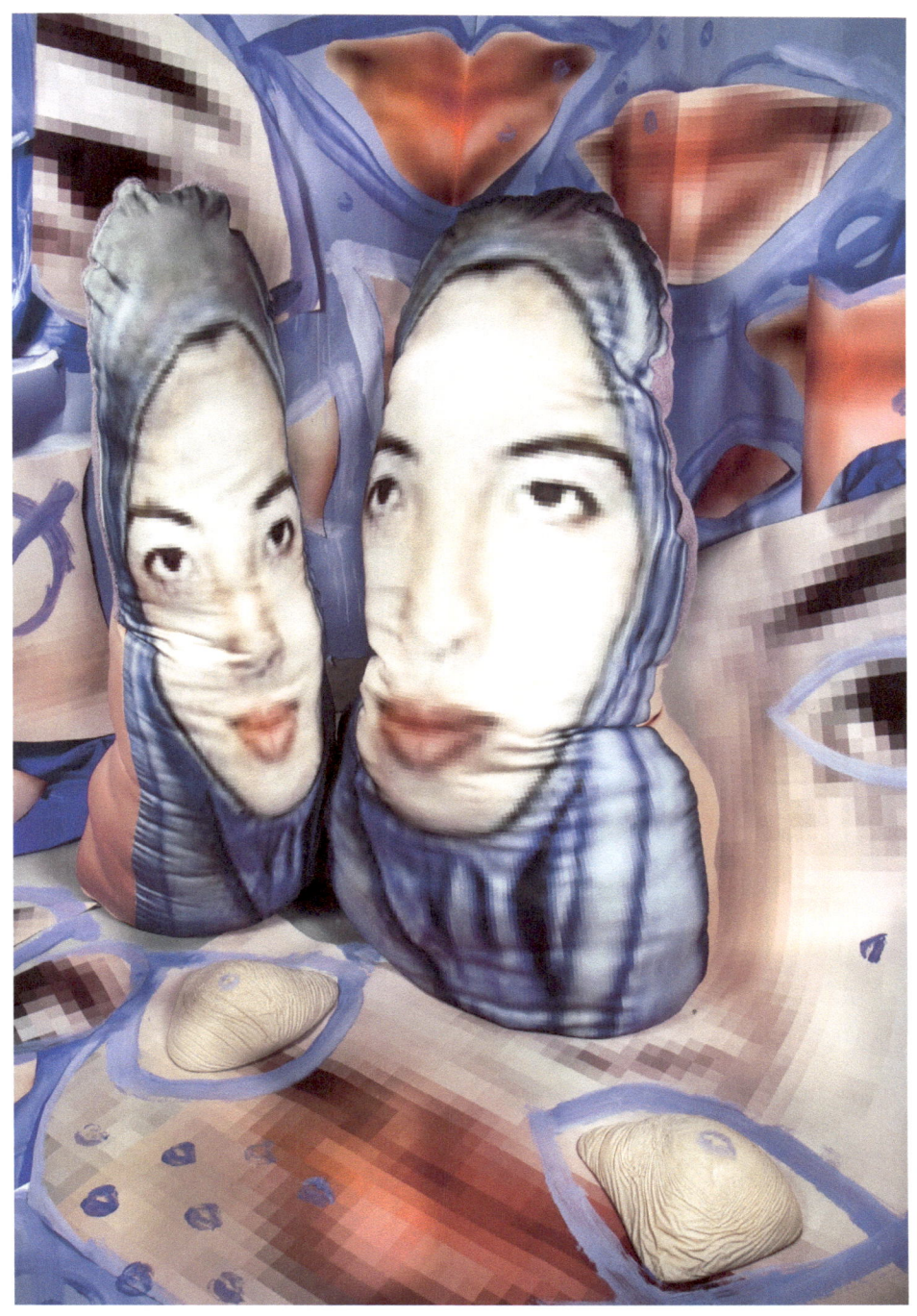

Delara (2), 2016
Archival pigment
print
40" x 27"

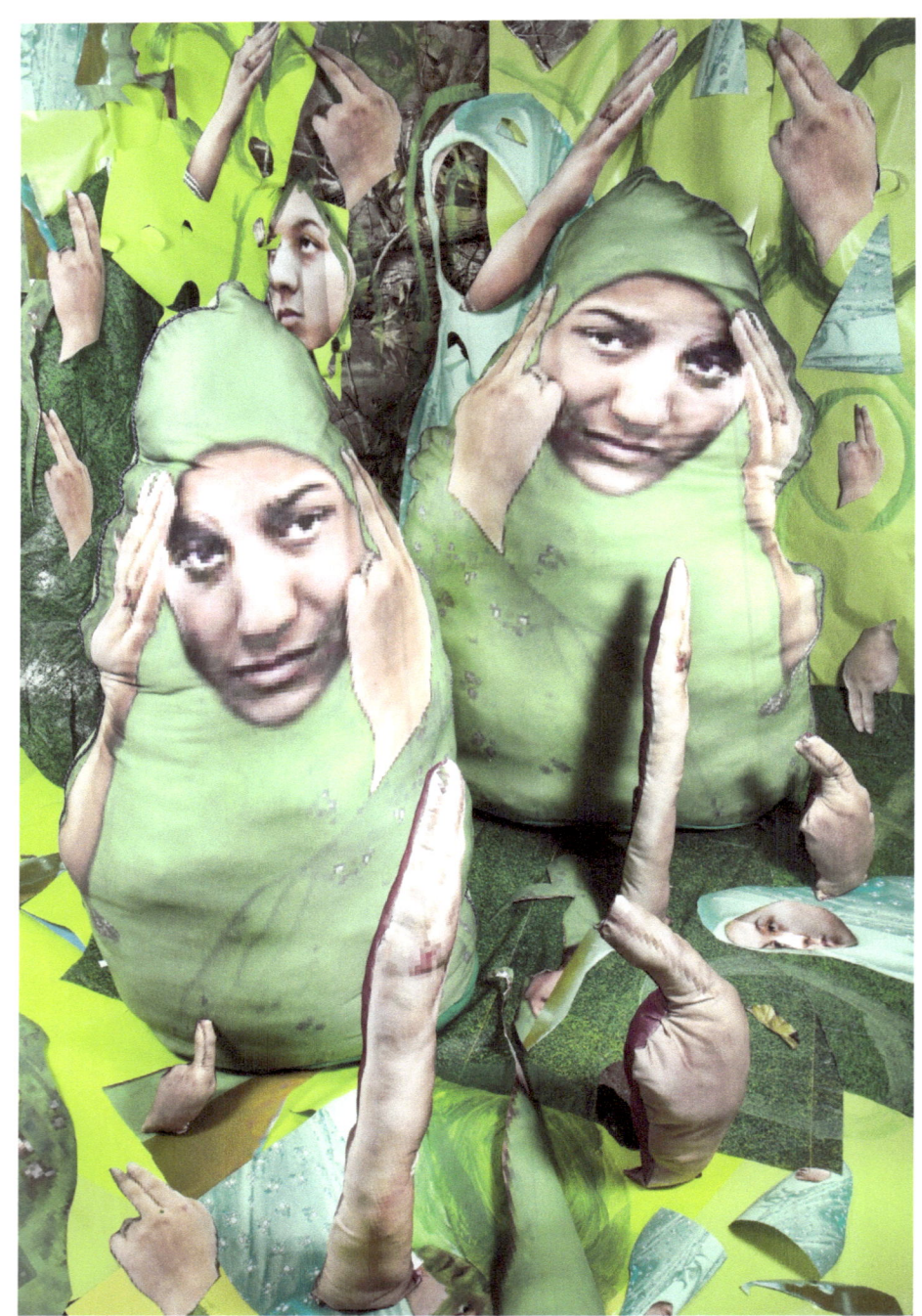

Reyhaneh (2), 2016
Archival pigment
print, 40" x 27"

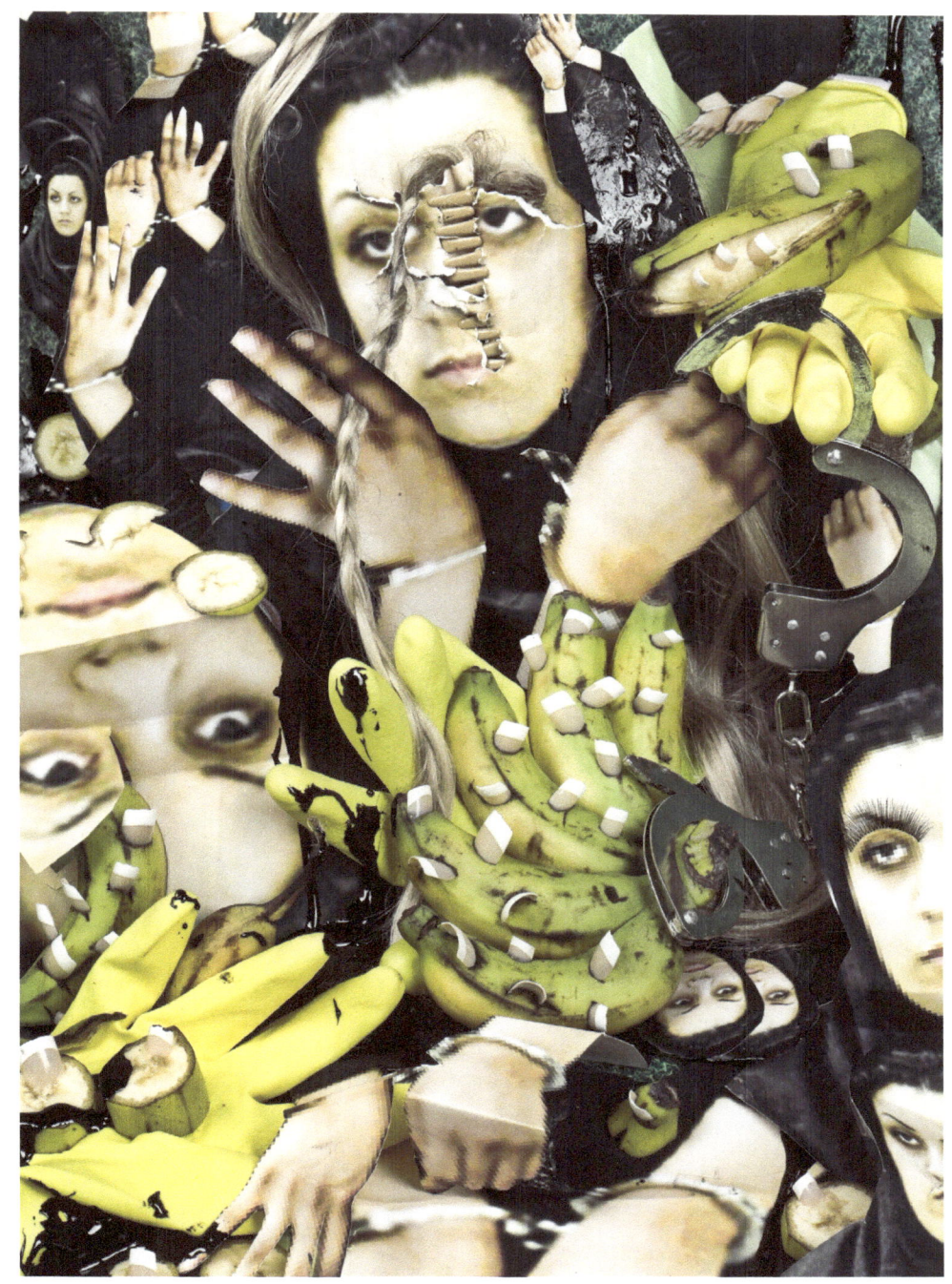

Reyhaneh, 2015
Archival pigment
print,
24" x 17"

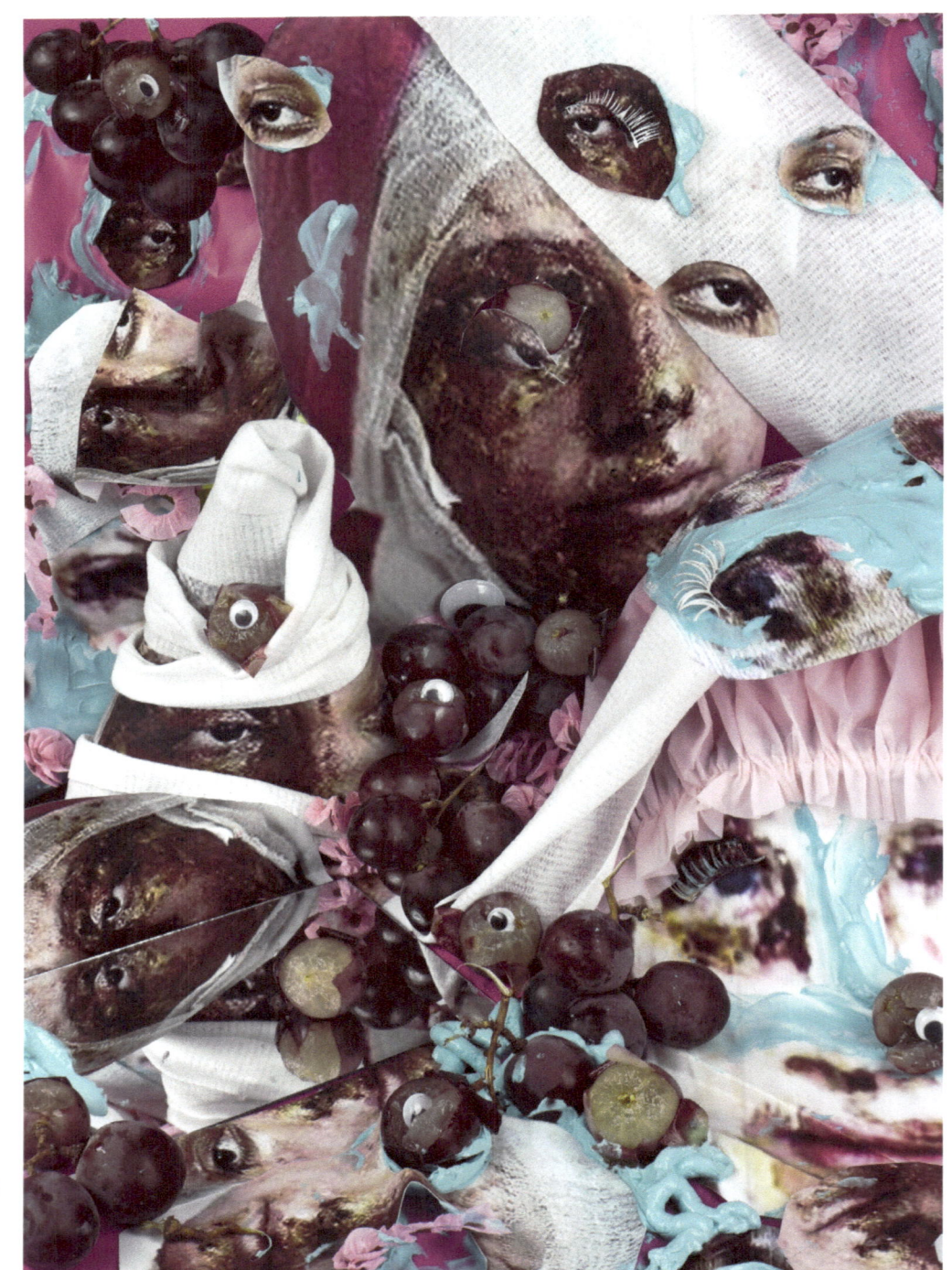

Vitriolic, 2015
Archival pigment
print,
24" x 17"

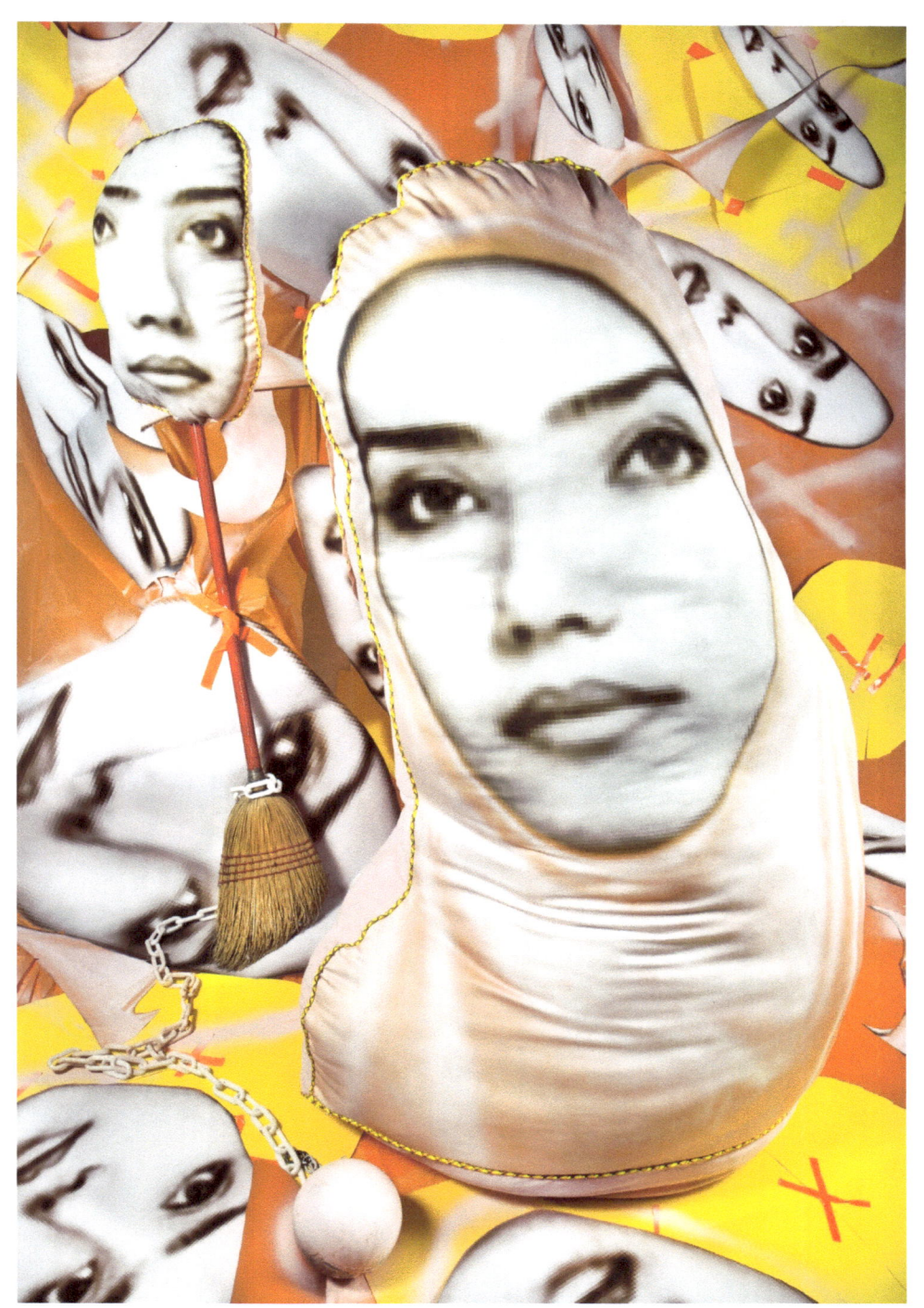

Taraneh, 2016
Archival pigment print,
40" x 27"

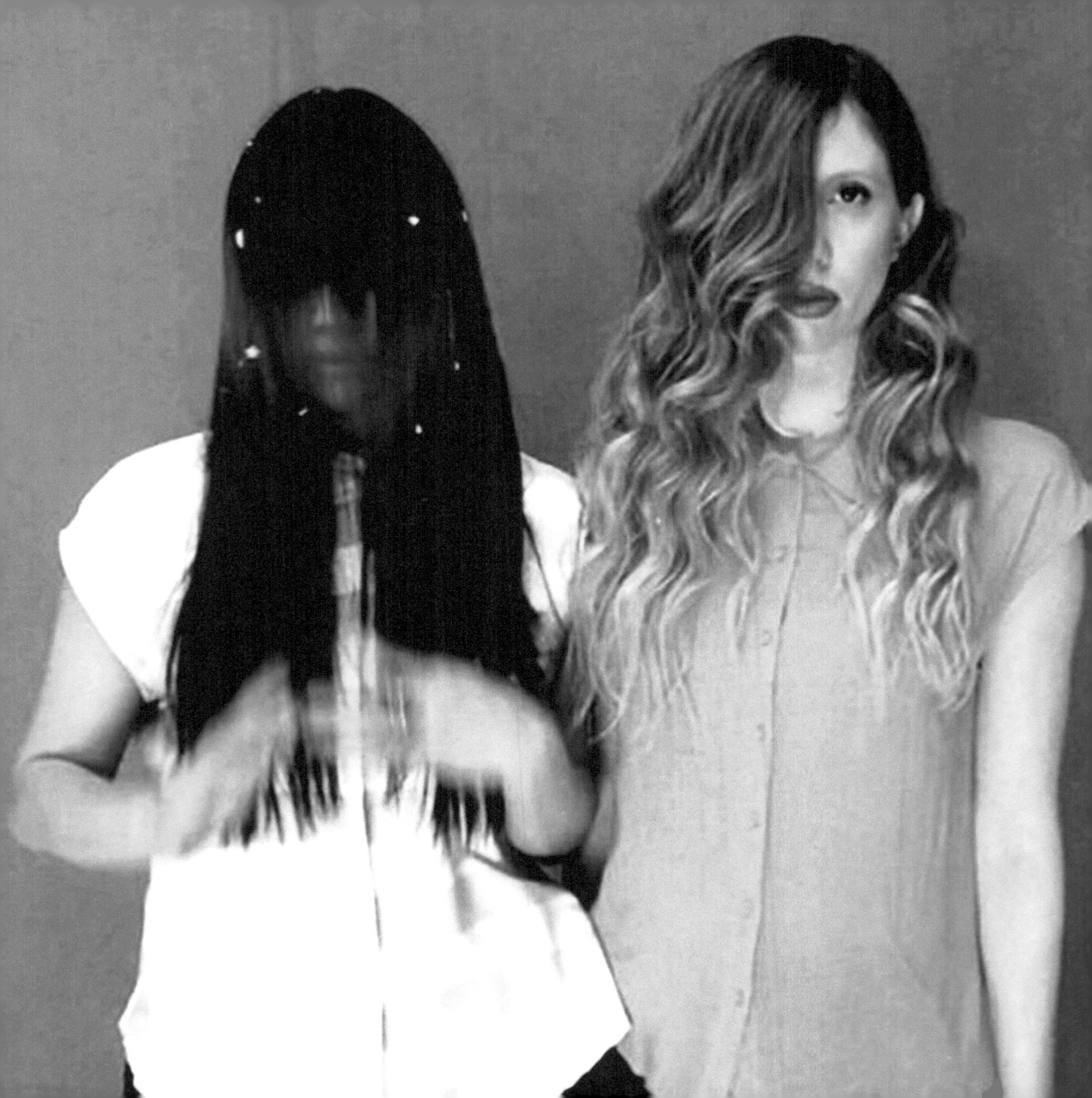

MODERN MAKERS

Modern Makers is an experimental arts program. We catalyze ideas and communities through experience design. We are a conduit for the creative community, bridging art, design, cuisine and culture with different social spheres. We activate small and big ideas, moving and changing with the landscape around us. Over the last five years we offered twelve events a year with a wide range of collaborations, audiences and visions. We hosted exhibitions in vacant spaces, research centers, warehouses and neighborhood centers. In 2016, we focused our programing to four events, greater impact in one spot with a wider sphere of influence.

Catherine Richards & Anh Tran
Co-Founders

Published in connection with exhibition:
Cincinnati 5: Stories & Stories

Co-curated by Catherine Richards, Anh Tran and Emily Moores
Modern Makers
March 17 - March 25, 2017

Editors: Keith Good, Elizabeth Tussey and Dan Murphy

All images of indivdual works of art are courtesy of the artists.

Modern Makers

2619 Glendora Ave.
Cincinnati, Ohio
http://modernmakers.org/

Distribution:
createspace
An Amazon Company
www.createspace.com